Mrs. Dunwoody's Excellent Instructions for Homekeeping

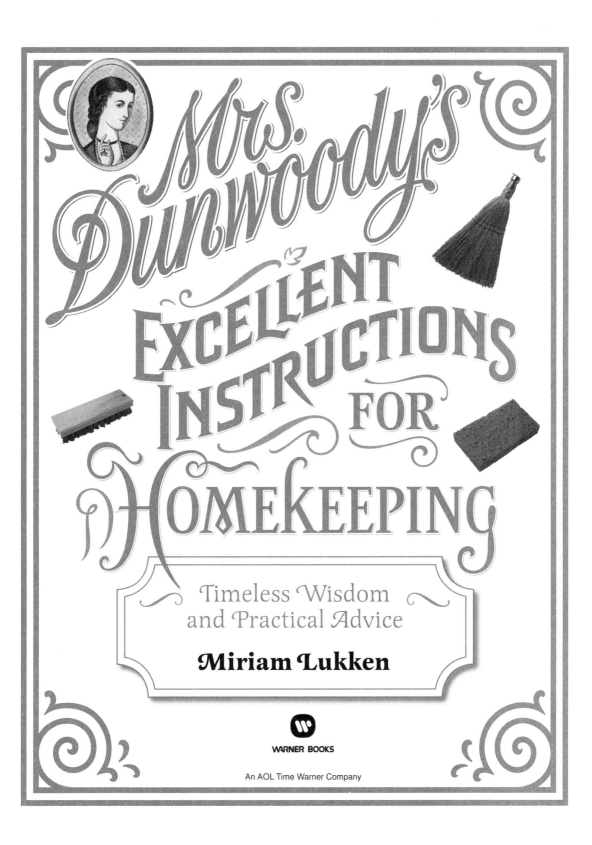

Mrs. Dunwoody's

Excellent Instructions for

Homekeeping

Timeless Wisdom and Practical Advice

Miriam Lukken

WARNER BOOKS

An AOL Time Warner Company

Warner Books, Inc., 1271 Avenue of the Americas,
New York, NY 10020

Visit our Web site at www.twbookmark.com.

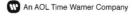 An AOL Time Warner Company

Printed in the United States of America
First Printing: April 2003
10   9   8   7   6   5   4   3   2   1

The Library of Congress Cataloging-in-Publication Data

Lukken, Miriam
Mrs. Dunwoody's excellent instructions for homekeeping : timeless
wisdom and practical advice / Miriam Lukken
p.   cm.
Includes bibliographical references and index.
ISBN 0-446-53013-1
1. Housekeeping.   I. Lukken, Miriam.   II. Title.
TX301.D88   2003
648—dc21
2002031112

Book design by Ralph Fowler
Illustrations on pages 37, 63, and 110–112 by Michael Gellatly

For Peter John,
the salt of the Southern earth.

Preface

Dear Reader:

What was an evening at home like, one hundred years ago? A simple homemade dinner enjoyed by the entire family at the kitchen table, where stories were told, lives were shared, and everyone listened to each other intently. This was followed by ajournment to the living room for games or study or reading by the firelight, and then early to bed, for the candle had faded, and day had turned to night.

Fast-forward to today, where speed is everything. A phone company promises to save you three seconds of your precious time to reach your caller. We fill our time with mindless television shows and are bombarded by advertisements appearing on buses, billboards, and T-shirts. In the grocery store, at the office, in traffic, in our homes, even in our microwaves, everything is fast and furious. It's as if we are under secret orders to *go* and *consume* and *live* at the fastest pace possible.

Our grandparents knew something we have forgotten—*Good things take time*. Love is slow and lasts, tenderness takes patience, wisdom comes with age, and the tall majestic oak tree outside of my window took eighty years to reach its glorious height. In the length of days comes understanding.

Someone once said when an old person dies, a library is lost.

How true! And yet we are too busy zooming into tomorrow to take time to look and listen to the past. Unlike our grandparents, we seem to be too distracted by life to *take the time* to teach and pass on our wisdom from one generation to the next.

Mrs. Dunwoody's Excellent Instructions for Homekeeping will help fill that void. This book is fashioned after the traditional notes nineteenth-century Southern women penned as a record of all they knew and thought meaningful. Practical and simple, reliable and trustworthy, these "receipt books" included everything from the nuts and bolts of day-to-day living to the rules of decent behavior in both company and conversation. These books were treasured and passed from one generation to the next. Part of what makes them so special is that most of what these women wrote is timeless and still very applicable to today.

Mrs. Dunwoody's Excellent Instructions for Homekeeping was written to provide today's reader with the advice and wisdom typical of these receipt books—practical information often forgotten or not explicitly explained, such as how to care for the sick, which seems to be such commonsense information that no one today thinks to teach others how to do it. Yet clearly it is sound advice worth preserving and passing on to the next generation. There are also blank pages in the back of the book for you to begin your own "receipt book" by recording the advice and wisdom from your own family.

These days, as people spend less and less time at home, more of us are turning to outside services to meet our basic needs such as food, laundry, cleaning, comfort, entertainment, and social interaction. This greatly reduces the chances of our homes nurturing us and being a source of comfort and contentment. Our homes are more beautiful, expensive, and luxurious than ever, with more material goods and conveniences than Mrs. Dunwoody could have ever imagined. We pay more for them, and spend less time in them, and so homekeeping as she defined it seems to be a lost art, and not very important anymore.

As you read Mrs. Dunwoody's advice, perhaps you will begin to feel a little daunted by her effortless perfection and tireless attention to every detail. But don't despair, dear reader, for Mrs. Dunwoody is actually *a character* based on my great-grandmother and other inspiring Southern women who held the art of homekeeping sacred. If we view Mrs. Dunwoody as a source of inspiration, rather than a yardstick to measure ourselves by, we suddenly become more like her than we ever thought possible. In fact, after looking through several of these receipt books and reading and sifting through my own family papers, I can imagine her to be as real as any willful, charming Southern Belle ever could be.

In the spring of 1866 Caroline Dunwoody sat down at her kitchen table and penned the first entry in a notebook that would take her over fifty years to complete. Fleshed out with borrowed wisdom, recipes, and household tips and etiquette from women of her day, she had begun her "receipt book" during the devastating days in Georgia immediately following the War between the States. Life was hard and rations were terribly scarce, but the women of that time were very enterprising when it came to necessities such as cooking and housekeeping. They began to recognize that their old way of life was gone forever, and the world was not likely to ever be the same.

Mrs. Dunwoody's advice and words of wisdom were meant to be passed down to each generation of women as they married and took up housekeeping—or "homekeeping" as she called it. Her instructions were meticulously written in her distinct style with such care and attention to detail that the notebook seemed almost holy, like a book with a soul of its own.

Mrs. Dunwoody was legendary in her family. Born in 1841 in Savannah, Georgia, and named Caroline (pronounced CARE-o-line) Anne Wylly, she was as smart as she was beautiful. Like most young women of any standing in her day, she attended a "finishing school" that provided a surprisingly well-rounded education. Her knowledge of geography and history was balanced by a perfect certainty of how to set an exquisite table and when and where to wear white gloves.

After completing her education, she met and married Charles Spalding Dunwoody, a promising young lawyer from South Carolina. They soon had six children and settled into a handsome, two-story house flanked with stately white columns in the west Georgia town of Glenn Cove. For a time, Charles Dunwoody represented the county in the state senate and house of representatives and was eventually elected judge of the circuit court. As Charles rose in stature, so did the couple. They were socially prominent and well known in the community for their hospitality. Since Mrs. Dunwoody had spent time in Washington, D.C., with her husband, she was considered "well traveled" by her contemporaries and therefore set the standards for much of the social scene in the small town.

Sadly, Judge Dunwoody died an untimely death after a brief illness, leaving his wife heartbroken. Like most widows of her day, she found her fortunes considerably reduced. To make ends meet in the devastating aftermath of the war, she began to take in boarders, rather than selling the large family home, as many of her friends were forced to do. It wasn't long before her home (known as Dunwoody House) had earned a sterling reputation and Caroline Dunwoody herself was respected as the most gracious and charming hostess in west Georgia.

During her "spare time," she also taught etiquette to the town's young ladies and gentlemen, and was eventually considered an authority on such things. It was during those days that Mrs. Dunwoody earned her nickname. "Big Mama" was certainly not a physical description of her, for she was a petite woman, only five feet in height with slender shoulders, eyes as clear as blue glass, and lovely black, glossy hair fashioned carefully on her head. Rather, "Big Mama" was a way of describing her heart. She lived life as a sort of celebration, every day. She was very practical, yet took great delight in the smallest detail that others would easily and often pass by. She truly believed that everyone had real worth and possessed something unique that she could uncover and learn from. She often wrote and spoke of finding the sacred in the everyday. In one of her many letters to her daughters, she noted, "One has to be in the same place every day, watch the sun rise from the same house, hear the same birds awaken each morning, to realize how inexhaustibly rich and different is sameness." And later, "Even the common articles made for daily use become endowed with beauty when they are loved. We must strive to see the goodness or usefulness in all things, taking nothing for granted. And we must approach every task as a blessing to be received, never as a chore." Those who knew her best describe a woman of elegance and effortless charm who dearly cherished her faith and was always attentive to the lives of those around her. She possessed a contagious passion for life and never met a stranger. She gave her motherly love to everyone. It is easy to understand why she was named Big Mama and acknowledged as a celebrity among her family and friends during her lifetime.

Due, perhaps, to the abject poverty that prevailed in the

South after the war, Mrs. Dunwoody kept notes on virtually every subject. Her instructions on how to treat a snakebite were followed by a cure for a broken heart and a recipe for collard greens. Every aspect of her life seemed sacred and worth preserving for future generations. After the war, books were scarce and paper even scarcer, so Big Mama felt more compelled than ever to complete her written instructions. In her notes, she wrote that homekeeping wasn't just a matter of cleaning a house; it was a matter of presentation, hospitality, entertaining, etiquette, organizing, letter writing, caring for loved ones, cooking, sewing, and just plain general information that made for a thoughtful, meaningful, and considered life.

Big Mama had a "method" for doing everything, and if this method was not observed, she became fierce. She, too, believed that the ordinary acts we practice every day at home are of more importance to the soul than their simplicity might suggest. "Taking care of our home enables us all to feel nurtured and safe; it brings comfort and solace both in the fruits of our labor and in the freedom it affords to experience life to its fullest. It is important work, and others will suffer if you do not attend to it properly," she wrote in one of her diaries. Big Mama was just as fussy about the manner in which things were done as she was about the substance of those things. She taught that women were not just doing chores, they were creating—creating a home, a place of security, warmth, contentment, and affection. A place where even the everyday things in our lives were held sacred and should therefore be cared for and treated in a special and orderly way. "Imagine if you lost every single one of your possessions for a month. Why, even a drinking glass would be meaningful to you at such a point! Consider how appreciative and happy you would *be if everything was then returned to you, just as it had been. Give it some thought," she wrote.*

In a letter to a grandchild Mrs. Dunwoody wrote, "Have nothing in your home that you do not know to be useful, or believe to be beautiful. Home is a sacred place for you and your family. Home interprets heaven. It is heaven for beginners. Take the time to come home to yourself, every day." She taught that home was where you came to rest, and so it should thereby be restorative. It should be a relief to come home at the end of the day, close the door behind you, and find things as they should be (and always have been). She taught that comfort and security are found in sameness. She truly believed that our own inner peace and happiness could be worked out by organizing our physical surroundings.

In our busy lives, parents seldom have time or thoughts to hand down the old-fashioned yet practical advice and wonderful wisdom of generations past and present. *Mrs. Dunwoody's Excellent Instructions for Homekeeping* offers this timeless information for readers. Her notes teach us that it *is possible* to enjoy the rituals of homekeeping. Perhaps through her eyes, we can discover the sacredness and beauty that exists in simple everyday things and rituals and begin to once again pass our own wisdom on to the next generation.

Truly, these notes are not simply about housekeeping tips and advice; they are also concerned with and encourage us in the larger issues of life. They act as a road map leading us to *a more considered and meaningful life* through nurturing a family and home, living respectfully, and passing on the legacy of love, hope, joy, and compassion to those around us. The simple, straightforward directions in Mrs. Dunwoody's notes were written to give hope that we can one day create a home nearly as wonderful and loving as I have imagined hers to be. This, dear reader, is for you my fondest hope. Happy homekeeping!

Miriam Lukken
LaGrange, Georgia
2003

Contents

Mrs. Dunwoody's Excellent Instructions for Homekeeping

Nobody knows of the work it makes
To keep the home together,
Nobody knows of the steps it takes,
Nobody knows—
but Mother.

Dear Precious Children,

This notebook is the result of a lifetime of experience, observation, and reading. I began these, my notes to you, in the year 1866. No untried theory is offered, and much labor and consideration have been bestowed upon these instructions. Consider that written learning is a fixed luminary, which after the cloud that had it hidden has passed away, is again bright in its proper station. So books are faithful repositories, which may be neglected or forgotten, but when opened again, will again impart instruction.

It is my sincere hope that you will find this notebook a companion of invaluable service, and a constant adviser, whose opinions may be trusted as entirely reliable. As you have heard me say countless times, "Method is the soul of management."

In these notes, I have endeavored to impart the knowledge necessary for keeping a neat, well-ordered home. But beyond that, I wish for you to understand the larger issues of homekeeping—creating an environment in which all family members grow and thrive, a place where each member may evolve to the full extent our Creator intended.

It is my belief that the housewife makes the home, and the home makes the nation. As Mrs. Julia Wright has written, children are born into a home, and they shall be in it all their lives. What this home makes them, they shall train up their future children to be—ennobled, or warped, as here they learned. They shall carry their energies and example into the world, for better or worse, as here was taught them. In this home children receive also their instruction; their worldly occupations are chosen, and fortunes laid up for them; their moral character is determined. You see thus that all the energies, the business, the industries, the inventions of the world, have really their center, their inception in the Home: It is the world's animate heart. Erase all homes, all home life, ties, needs, joys, and how long would the wheels of labor and commerce move on? How important, then, is every Home! What a tremendous responsibility surrounds its founding! How needful to count the cost!

As you go forth into the world to begin the prodigious work of life, it is my greatest wish that you find success and happiness in creating your own home. I have no doubt in your ability to accomplish this. For in all of you, I find that the great lesson I have striven to impart to you, is well learned—the most exquisite pleasure in life, is giving pleasure to others. As the good Lord taught us, the finest quality of greatness is service.

And so I remain,

Your Loving and Devoted Big Mama Dunwoody

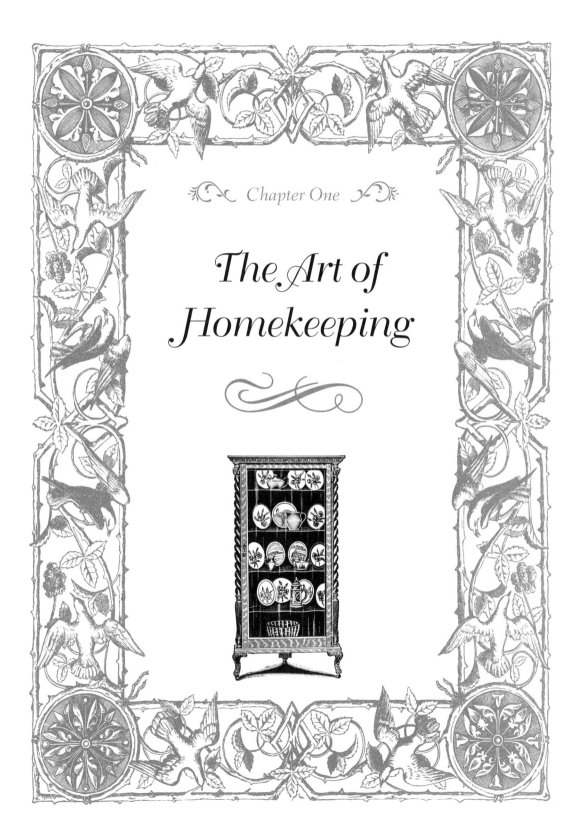

Chapter One

The Art of Homekeeping

The Art of Homekeeping

All of us carry in our hearts and minds the image of our ideal home, realized or not. It is a place where we feel we belong, a rightness, at-homeness, a knitting together of self and world. Home is a place to become yourself, to rest and surrender all pretense. As Dear Mother used to say, "Home is the place where you can restore your mind, body, and soul." It is a source of emotional nourishment. It's where you can close a door and open your heart. If there is any meaning to existence, we are surely closest to it there.

We often take our homes for granted. But when we steep ourselves in our home, a deep sense of place begins to emerge. Life becomes more meaningful. We begin to have a greater spiritual awareness of what our home is and should be. Perhaps our most inspiring thought is that our homes, if we are to live well in them, require and deserve a lifetime of the most careful attention. A home absorbs caretaking like a sponge. All the hours we spend tending to it are never in vain, for everything we give to our home, is in turn, given back to us. Our homes will be only as generous and nurturing as the effort we invest in them.

How can we create this special place? A home that rises up to meet us when we come through the door. One that calls out to our soul and draw us in like a magnet. A home that calms, soothes, rejuvenates, and restores. Let us begin by considering the five senses: sight, sound, touch, taste, and smell.

Colors have a grand effect on our nerves and should be considered carefully. What colors are pleasing to our sight? A bold and bright cranberry damask wallpaper with Copenhagen blue trim, or the quiet, soothing tones of a sea-foam green or pale yellow goldenrod? The colors in our rooms should reflect what is most pleasing to our eye. Color strongly affects mood, so pay attention to the way various colors stir your emotions. If you want to make a strong statement in a room, choose strong colors. For a soothing effect in a room, choose pastels or cool colors.

Experiment with color combinations. Some of my favorite color combinations include cream and violet, or rose blush and chocolate accented with sage green, or cream white with turkey red. Maroon and pallid sea green is beautiful also. Ask yourself, "What do I want to look at every day?"

Papered walls can achieve very specific effects. Vertical strips make a room seem taller. In a small room a large pattern can be overpowering, but in a big room it often has a cozy feel. The less dense the pattern, the greater the effect. A dense pattern, even if it is small in scale, creates a busy feeling within a room.

There is no right or wrong in choosing colors as long as the occupant is happy with the results. We must, however, give careful consideration to these color choices, because color alone can completely transform a home.

Also to consider is the display of the room. The most successful decorative plans result from well-chosen focal points such as fireplaces or large pieces of furniture or artwork. Large mirrors dramatically increase the feel of size within a room. One must be careful not to clutter the room, which reduces the impact of a room's finer features. Is there simply too much in the room? With respect given to the smaller pleasures of day-to-day living, can we make it more pleasing by removing or by adding something? Do we prefer a simplistic look, a mere table, chair, and lamp, or a more complex, intriguing mix of books, antiques, and collectibles dispersed creatively among several seating areas in the room? Do we wish to live in light and airy rooms or cozy and comfortable ones? What is the purpose of each room: grand social occasions or relax-

"Home is the definition of God."
—Emily Dickinson

ing family times together? Is it a welcoming home full of graceful details?

How does smell affect our homes? Have you experienced the stirring in your soul when some pleasing aroma takes you back to a charming memory? The mouthwatering smell of a freshly baked loaf of bread in the oven, or the soothing, fragrant mixture of lavender and magnolias in the bedroom. Smell can be a powerful tool in the creation of a nurturing and pleasing home.

You most likely don't notice the smell of your own home until you return to it from an extended stay or vacation. Take care to notice the smells in your home. Is it musty and stale, or perhaps sterile with a lingering scent of ammonia? Or is it filled with the faintly sweet smell of flowers cut fresh from the garden? We can find pleasing scents and aromas for our homes by using fresh plants and flowers, fresh fruit zest, or candles, and incense. On the washstand a bowl of lavender-scented water calms the senses and soothes the nerves, while a basket of perfumed French soaps and sachets next to the towels in the washroom creates an oasis of purity and beauty. We can remove unpleasant odors from our home by keeping them clean and free of clutter, and by airing them out regularly by opening the windows.

How does our home feel? Cozy and soft? Grand and exciting? Do we wish to live in an opulent atmosphere, or a simple one? Are there many accommodating, inviting pieces of furniture to retire on or merely a few ladder-back chairs with little else for resting? Are there good books, plush rugs, and luxurious chairs and sofas? Is the lighting bright and plentiful, or subtle from a small table lamp? Are the bedrooms dark and dreary, or sunny, bright, and cheery? What is the feeling we wish to create upon entering a room?

What are the sounds of our everyday lives? The sweet giggles of young children along with the barks of a favorite dog? Wind chimes on the front porch or lovely music drifting through the house from the front parlor? What are the sounds that our ears long to hear? Laughter of friends, or a soft piano? Or is silence golden?

Taste. What do we wish to serve to our favorite guests? Something simple and sweet, or exotic and special? A "house specialty" that everyone looks forward to? Perhaps a mouthwatering rabbit stew that entices the appetites of everyone who enters the front door? Or more simply, just plain yet nourishing food served in a grand style. What foods will we offer for the pleasure of our family and guests?

All of these notions deserve our careful consideration as we strive to make our home the most special place in our lives. Home reflects the creativity, serenity, and beauty we hold dear. It should restore our souls. Home should be the place where we can grow, and thrive, and live and love, to the fullest extent.

A Little Common Sense

Our family members will carry the atmosphere we create in our homes for the rest of their lives.

Homekeeping is a fine art. It grasps with one hand beauty, with the other utility; it has its harmonies like music, and its order like the stars in their courses. I fear really good homekeeping—which exhibits itself not in occasional entertainment or a handsome parlor, but in good housekeeping which extends from the attic to the cellar, and through every hour in the year—is far from common.

As Dear Mother always used to say, organization has more benefits than mere efficiency. I heartily agree. Knowing your life and home are in order reduces strife and anxiety, and increases confidences. In short, establishing your own routine for tackling domestic chaos makes the task less burdensome. And everyone feels the effects of that.

Homekeeping is an ongoing art, a process, not an end product. It will never be "all done." Bathrooms, clothes, and dishes, once clean, have a way of getting dirty again. But home is meant to be lived in, in the fullest, most po-

Recipe for a Happy Home

Half a cup of friendship, and a cup of thoughtfulness,
creamed together with a pinch of powdered tenderness,
very lightly beaten in a bowl of loyalty
with a cup of faith, one of hope, and one of charity.
Be sure to add a spoonful of gaiety that sings,
also the ability to laugh at little things.
Moisten with sudden tears of heartfelt sympathy,
bake in a good-natured oven and serve repeatedly.

tentially fulfilling way for everyone in it. That means that every room does not need to be picture perfect and waiting for a perfect display, but rather, each room has a sense of order and calmness to it. The home looks like someone lives there, without appearing messy or cluttered. There is an order and a method which is followed faithfully. There is a "place" for everything and everything *is in* its place. There is a "domestic calendar" for cleaning and chores. And that, my dears, is the first lesson in the "art of homekeeping."

The Homemaker's Daily Routine

It is my belief that a meaningful day has its roots firmly established in routine. I have found that if I rise early and give my day to God in prayer, I am assured of an orderly and well-managed home. The importance of early rising cannot be emphasized enough. Usually the quietest portion of the day, this time alone is essential for ordering activities and collecting one's thoughts. It can become a treasured retreat of serenity that prepares and equips one for whatever the day may hold.

Just as there is a reassuring rhythm to the seasons, the wind, the sea, and the beating of our hearts, so should there be a rhythm to our lives. It is the rhythm of routine which is, by far not dull and ordinary, but freeing and comforting in that it allows us a sense of calm and order which we can depend on to become the foundation, or the starting point for fulfilling our highest and most creative purpose. It is out of this "rhythm of routine" that order is established. Order is heaven's first law; without it, a home and its occupants cannot realize their full potential. When we make conscious decisions about the order in which we shall tend to our duties and live our lives, everyone in the home thrives. Children

The Housemaid's Routine

Circa 1885

Rise at 6:00 A.M.

Clean grates by 7:00.

Open shutters by 7:15.

Sweep rooms by 7:30.

Dust and have downstairs rooms ready by 8:00.

Cook should have breakfast prepared by 8:00.

Have your own breakfast until 8:30.

Prepare all ready to go upstairs by 9:00.

Turn down all beds to air out and open all windows by 9:30.

Clear away things, tidy up, empty slops, and change water by 10:00.

Make beds by 11:00.

Sweep and tidy bedrooms by 11:30.

Check with Cook to see lunch ready by 12:00 P.M.

Have your own lunch finished by 12:45.

Dust and lay all smooth by 1:00.

Clean yourself ready for Needlework or whatever may be required of you by 1:30.

especially find comfort in repetition, routines, and order. But it does not come naturally, so it must first be *imposed* on them.

A Word about Children and Housekeeping

"A place for everything, and everything in its place." Well and truly, there is a time for certain duties, and the homekeeper must see that there is no infringement of the laws that are laid down for the household. Children cannot too soon be taught the importance of order, neatness, and economy. A habit of system must be early formed, and will prove a blessing through life. Habit is a cable; and if we weave a thread of it each day, it becomes so strong we cannot break it.

An ill-governed household, where there is neither system, order, neatness, nor frugality, is a bad school for children. If you set an example of carelessness, do not blame your children for following it. Children should be taught to put things back in their places as soon as they are old enough to use them, and if each member of the family were to observe this simple rule, the house would never get much out of order.

The Daily Cleanup

I suggest that after breakfast, you should begin with the daily cleanup. Take a twenty-minute walk around the house with a basket hung on your arm and a dustcloth in your hand. The basket, of course, is to gather up the small items that are out of place, carrying them with you until you reach the place where they belong. This saves endless trips back and forth from one room to another. As you go, you will gather up the jacket or shawl that was left on a chair, and carry it over your arm until you reach the owner's bedroom. Start in the living room, and wind up in the bedrooms, opening windows as you go to fill the house with wonderfully refreshing air, and making the beds as you come to them. Now you have a house in perfect order, early in the day, and you can move on to the major task for the day—laundering, marketing, the thorough cleaning of a specific room, or whatever the day demands. When you have finished your primary duties of the day, it is so pleasant to know that the house is *already* in perfect order, and you need only attend to your own needs or those of your family.

The Domestic Calendar

Dear daughters, I encourage you to establish a daily, weekly, monthly, and yearly housekeeping routine. This is the most important thing you can do to make your home work well. Do everything in its time and place, and you will not only accomplish more, but have far more leisure time than those who are always hurrying.

To develop a set of routines for yourself, consider all the household work you have and divide it into portions that must be daily, weekly, monthly or seasonally, and yearly or less often. There should be a regular time for everything. A regular month for housecleaning and sewing and mending, for planting and harvesting the garden. A regular week for putting by winter bedding, and clothes in big chests—all mended and clean before put by; a regular day for sweeping, dusting, and cellar cleaning; a regular hour for cooking and baking; a regular minute for rising and retiring, for breakfast and dinner and tea. Give our maid Sallie Anne the day of the week and the hour of the day and she knows what we are doing here at home. That is the way to get through. Nothing is forgotten: nothing is left undone. This, for instance, is the week when the herbs are cut and dried, while they are green and strong. This week Sallie Anne washes the blankets and suns the heavy quilts, and I clean, mend, and put by the winter clothing. In the fall it will be a pleasure to take out clean whole things which have lain packed away neatly, in sweet-smelling lavender.

Certainly it would be prudent to establish a "homekeeping notebook." In this manner you may save yourself time by recording the particular details of a job or chore, apportion time efficiently, and report how and when you cleaned special items, and what you used, to avoid trial and error the next time. Find the patterns and habits that work best for you and your home. Record them in your notebook and follow them year after year. Of course order and cleanliness should not cost more than the value they bring to your home and family, but an established outline will ultimately give you a sense of contentment.

Order is a mainspring in housework. Indeed, an example of habit and order is one of the nicest dowries a woman can give her daughters: one to prolong her life, to build up her home, and be always a source of comfort to herself and family. Good habits, which bring our lower passions and appetites under automatic control, leave our natures free to explore the larger experiences of life.

Here is my list of daily, weekly, and monthly chores. I hope it will inspire you as you create your own domestic calendar.

"My idea of house cleaning is to sweep the room with a glance."
—AUNT MIDDLE MARY

Daily Cleaning Chores

Make beds.
Prepare meals and clean afterward.
Tidy up rooms and put everything back into its proper place.
Put soiled clothes in laundry and hang up other clothes.

Clean or put out tablecloth and kitchen towels.
Tidy the bathrooms and put out clean towels and necessary
   toiletries.
Clean floors in kitchen and dining rooms.
Do marketing.
Take out the trash.
Complete day-of-the-week chore.

Day-of-the-Week Chores

Washing on Monday.
Ironing on Tuesday.
Sewing on Wednesday.
Marketing on Thursday.
Cleaning on Friday.
Baking on Saturday.
Rest on Sunday.

Weekly Cleaning Chores

Marketing for food and nonfood items.
Wash all floors.
Tend to laundry.
Wipe down all surfaces such as doorknobs and cabinet
   handles.
Dust all furniture and objects.
Clean bathrooms very thoroughly.
Clean kitchen, scrub counters, sinks, and floor.
Change the bed linens.
Clean garbage receptacle.
Wash combs and brushes.

Monthly Cleaning Chores

Wash or air feather pillows.
Wash mirrors.
Wash windows inside.

Wax floors.
Organize drawers.
Clean pantry.
Clean oven and stove.
Organize closets.
Wash or wax woodwork.

Fall and Spring Cleaning

There should be a general thorough and complete housecleaning twice every year—in the spring and fall. Always begin upstairs, clean and put everything to rights, move as much furniture as possible and clean under and behind it. Then descend to the lower floors.

Accessories are often the most important part in giving personality to the home. Most homes, after years of random accumulations, get cluttered with accessories that add nothing to the decoration. Open shelves with knickknacks, books, hobby items, pictures, lamp bases, ashtrays, silver, copper, glass, and other table decorations may add charm, or clutter, depending on selection and use. Do not hoard items you are not using. Give away as many items as necessary and avoid thinking, "I'll save this for another day; I may need it." The truth is that those types of items are almost never used (and in my case, I usually can't seem to find them if I ever do think I need them). You will feel blessed by giving away items or clothes that you are not using, and it is the law of the spiritual realm that what we give away comes back to bless us at least equally and often, many times more.

Guard against monotony by rotating living room accessories with the seasons. Use richly colored pottery pieces for fall; warm-colored lamps and handsome oil paintings for winter; gay fragile vases and a group of vivid watercolors for spring; and crystal flower containers, ashtrays, and lamps for summer.

To obtain a cool look for summer, minimize accessories. If

practical, rugs should be taken up and floors covered with colored linen or cotton summer rugs, or just left bare. Replace winter draperies with light summer drapes or perhaps sheer white curtains. Slipcovers in cool colors should cover upholstered furniture, both as a summer change and a protection against dust and fading. Furniture should be rearranged so that chairs catch the summer breezes. Potted palms, exotic orchids, and comfortable furnishings crafted of white wicker are ideal. The fireplace may be whitewashed in the summer. (Warm water will remove it in the fall.) Decorative branches or evergreens may be substituted for logs. Lamp shades should be changed to white or light colors. Heavy oil paintings and tapestries may be removed, and watercolors or mirrors hung in their place. A sense of bareness is also a sense of coolness. Your family will appreciate your decorative touches which, like the change of the seasons, renew, invigorate, and delight.

I have found that during my spring and fall cleaning, it helps to whitewash at least one of those times. It freshens and purifies and makes the family feel rejuvenated by all being neat, clean, and in its proper order.

For Fall Cleaning

Clean and clear out cellar and attic.
Wash all blankets and sun the heavy quilts.
Clean, mend, and put by furs, thick clothes,
winter hats, and winter bedding.
Replace summer curtains with winter drapes.
Remove, clean, and store summer slipcovers.
Wax the furniture.
Clean lamps and shades.
Hang carpets for a good beating and
then sun them for a day.
Sun and air mattresses and pillows.
Turn mattresses.

Domestic Calendar Notes on Chores and Cleaning

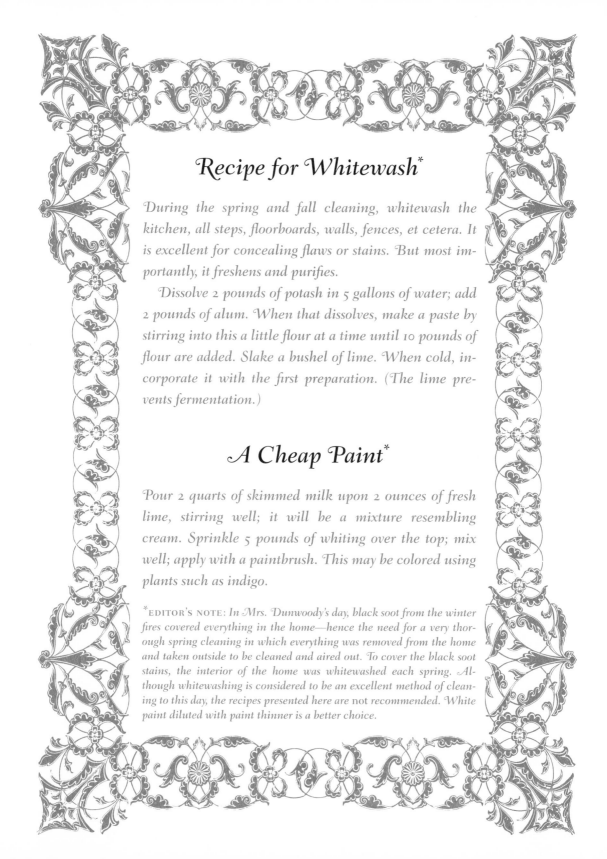

Recipe for Whitewash*

During the spring and fall cleaning, whitewash the kitchen, all steps, floorboards, walls, fences, et cetera. It is excellent for concealing flaws or stains. But most importantly, it freshens and purifies.

Dissolve 2 pounds of potash in 5 gallons of water; add 2 pounds of alum. When that dissolves, make a paste by stirring into this a little flour at a time until 10 pounds of flour are added. Slake a bushel of lime. When cold, incorporate it with the first preparation. (The lime prevents fermentation.)

A Cheap Paint*

Pour 2 quarts of skimmed milk upon 2 ounces of fresh lime, stirring well; it will be a mixture resembling cream. Sprinkle 5 pounds of whiting over the top; mix well; apply with a paintbrush. This may be colored using plants such as indigo.

*EDITOR'S NOTE: In Mrs. Dunwoody's day, black soot from the winter fires covered everything in the home—hence the need for a very thorough spring cleaning in which everything was removed from the home and taken outside to be cleaned and aired out. To cover the black soot stains, the interior of the home was whitewashed each spring. Although whitewashing is considered to be an excellent method of cleaning to this day, the recipes presented here are not recommended. White paint diluted with paint thinner is a better choice.

For Spring Cleaning

> Move all furniture away from the walls.
> Clean floors under furniture and
>   whitewash or wipe down all walls.
> Go through all drawers, giving away any
>   unused articles.
> Throw out worn-out articles.
> Clean chandeliers and lanterns.
> Have the piano cleaned and tuned.
> Dust and air the books.
> Clean and polish silver, brass, and copper.
> Wash windows on the outside.
> Hang carpets for a good beating, and then sun them for a day.
> Whitewash kitchen area, pantry, back porch, and steps.
> Sun and air mattresses and pillows.
> Turn mattresses.

Mrs. Dunwoody's Notes for Planning a Superior Day

Of all the many questions folks have asked me through the years, I suppose "How do you find the time to do it all?" is the one they ask the most. I had never really put much thought to the answer before now, but as I ponder the advice I would like to pass on to you, my precious children, I suppose a few hints do begin to take shape.

Perhaps most important:

1. *Make a plan for your day.* Otherwise you'll find your-self making the fatal mistake of dealing primarily with problems rather than opportunities. Start each day by making a general schedule, with particular emphasis on two or three

major things you would like to accomplish—including things that will achieve long-term goals. Each day you need to have a destination in mind.

2. *Concentrate.* I have observed that *concentration* is a key aspect of effective use of time. The amount of time spent on a chore seems not to matter as much as the amount of *uninterrupted* time. Few problems can resist an all-out attack. If you dedicate fifteen solid, uninterrupted minutes to an immense task, it will not seem so overwhelming the next time you return to it. Keeping this in mind inspires us to sally forth and do battle upon our chores.

3. *Learn to rest and catch your breath.* To work for long periods of time without taking a break is *not* the most effective use of your time. In fact, when you labor too long without rest, your work suffers for it and you end up spending more time to complete your task. You, and you alone, know what a good amount of time is before a break. Take that time, before energy decreases, boredom sets in, or physical stress and tension accumulate. Sometimes changing from a standing position to a sitting position is all that is needed to maintain your effectiveness. But whatever the need, do not underestimate, or feel guilty about your need for a rest. It is not a poor use of your time to rest; on the contrary, being refreshed increases your productivity.

4. *Don't procrastinate.* It is the thief of time. Start off your day by doing the most unpleasant chore first. (It's usually something that takes minimal effort—an apology, a long-overdue thank-you, or an annoying chore.) Whatever it is, do it before you begin your usual morning routine. You will get such a feeling of exhilaration knowing that although the day is only half an hour along, you have already conquered the most troublesome task of the day. As Emerson said,

"Guard well your spare moments. They are like uncut diamonds. Discard them and their value will never be known. Improve them and they will become the brightest gems in a useful life."

5. *Sift and sort.* Don't assume the most important matters will "float to the top." You must sort through the clutter of the day and categorize. Ask yourself, "What needs immediate action, and what can I tend to by the fire's light this evening in my favorite chair?" Remember, you can think of only one thing at a time, and you can work on only one task at a time, so focus all your attention on the most important one. Say to yourself, "Is this the *most* important thing that needs doing right now?" If not, then do the thing that is.

6. *Strive for excellence, not perfection.* Perfection does not exist. Perhaps this is one of the most important things I can teach you, my precious children, for the women in my

A Little Common Sense

To keep your sanity and save time in the morning, set the breakfast table with dishes and silverware, coffeepot, et cetera, and nonperishable items the night before. Also, take the time to put the other items you will need for the next day (papers, clothes, and so on) in a place where you will be sure to find them upon arising.

family seem not to realize that *there is a great difference in striving for excellence and striving for perfection.* The first is attainable, gratifying, and healthy. The second is impossible, frustrating, and neurotic (not to mention obnoxious). It is also a terrible waste of time.

Did you know, dear children, that when the inscriber of the Declaration of Independence made two errors of omission, he inserted the missing letters between the lines? If this is acceptable (almost charming) to the document that gave birth to American freedom, surely it would be acceptable in a letter that will be read merely once by your fussy Aunt Hortince!

7. *Never lose sight of the "big picture."* Some things need only five minutes or so, tending to a day, while others may need five hours. But if you can try to maintain a perspective, and remember that people (especially children) are *always* more important than things, you will do well in life.

After all, *today* is all we ever have to work with. Don't borrow trouble from tomorrow. Take it minute by minute, wisely, and you will succeed. As you've often heard me say, "Trust in God and do the next thing."

"Prayer should be the key of the morning and the lock of the night."

—OWEN FELLTHAM

Chapter Two

The Cares of House and Home

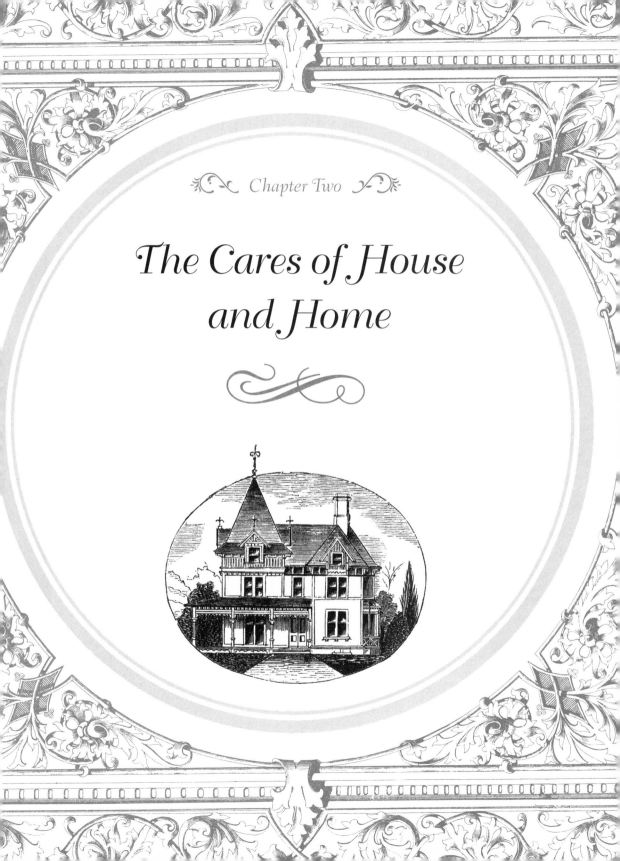

Judicious Cleaning Hints

EDITOR'S NOTE: *Although these hints are more than a century old, they are still very effective today; some of these cleaning products even work better than today's counterparts. They are cheaper and, in some instances, safer, as most of them do not have harmful chemicals in them.*

The basic cleaners for around the house are soap, warm or boiling water, vinegar, baking soda, household ammonia, and salt. These ingredients will effectively clean all but the nastiest jobs.

When cleaning any surface, always start with the gentlest solution. If it works, there is no reason to use anything stronger, for it may damage the surface over time. If the surface to be cleaned can be washed, try soap and plain old hot water. Carry a bucket of hot water with you and a good heavy washrag to wipe down the surface. If something stronger is needed, here are several options:

☞ *Vinegar (white distilled).* No kitchen should be without the very best cleaner of all. Its secret weapon is its acidity, which is just strong enough to cut through dirt and grease without damaging the surface. It works best for cleaning windows, cutting grease and grime, and freshening the air. Never use apple cider vinegar, for its brown color may stain.

☞ *Baking soda.* A gentle abrasive good for cleaning counters, pots, and pans. It is also an effective deodorizer for shoes, iceboxes, and other strong odors around the house.

☞ *Ammonia.* Ammonia is good for many jobs in the kitchen including removing wax from floors, cutting grease, and washing windows. Its powerful smell can be somewhat tamed with lemon juice. Ammonia is very strong and should always be diluted with water.

☞ *Salt.* Good for cleaning up oven spills, scouring, or removing burned-on foods.

Nonpareil Cleaning Solutions

Miss Sallie Anne's All-Purpose Household Cleaner

½ cup vinegar
1 cup clear ammonia
¼ cup baking soda
1 gallon hot water

—————

Mix all together in a bucket. This formula will most likely serve all of your household cleaning needs. Mop or wipe surfaces until clean.

Excellent Cleaner for Very Nasty Chores

1 cup baking soda
1 gallon hot water
1 cup clear ammonia
1 cup vinegar
1 tablespoon grated soap

—————

Using a bucket, dissolve the baking soda into the hot water. Add the ammonia, vinegar, and soap flakes. Stir to mix. This works well on toilets, tiles, radiators, and floors. Rinse with water.

Miss Lucinda's Lemon Furniture Polish

———

Add 1 teaspoon of lemon oil, or the juice of 1 lemon, to 2 cups of mineral oil. Apply with a soft cloth and buff until you can see your reflection.

The Chimney Soot Remover

———

Mix 1 cup of salt with 1 cup of zinc oxide powder. Mix and sprinkle on the fire to keep the flue clean and smoke-free. A handful of salt thrown on a blazing-hot fire also works well.

To Prevent Mildew

———

Wiping down surfaces with vinegar helps prevent mildew because acid kills mildew fungus.

Drain Declogger

———

Pour ¼ cup baking soda down the drain. Then follow with ¼ cup vinegar. Close the drain and let it sit until the bubbling has stopped. Then follow with a bucket of boiling water.

Cleaning Silver

———

Silver requires more care than any other household metal because sulfur compounds in the air cause it to tarnish. If soap is not rinsed off well after washing, the silver tarnishes more quickly. Silver bags and chests sometimes are treated with various salts to retard tarnishing. Air should be kept away from stored silver as much as possible to reduce the need for frequent polishing. But of course, you may wish to keep your finer, larger pieces, such as the tea and coffee service, on display in the dining room or parlor.

To clean silver, fill an aluminum vessel with hot water. (It will be corroded in the process. Clean the aluminum by boiling in a weak vinegar solution to keep it bright and active.) Add to the hot water in the vessel a teaspoon of salt and a teaspoon of baking soda for each quart of water. Bring the water to a boil and drop in the pieces of silver. If the water is kept boiling, the silver will be brighter. In a few seconds— the time depends on the degree of tarnish—the silver will be bright. It must then be washed in mild soapy water, rinsed, and polished with a soft, dry cloth.

To clean silver cutlery quickly, put an aluminum pan in a large sink and place the silverware in it. Cover all with boiling water and 3 tablespoons of baking soda. Soak for 10 minutes.

Polishing Glassware

Using a thin paste of baking powder and water, rub into the glass. Rinse well and dry with a soft cloth to create a bright shine.

Cobweb Remover

Use feathers to remove those unsightly cobwebs that cling to the upper walls and ceilings. I have found that peacock feathers work best, which I get from our neighbor Mr. Quartermane. But turkey, duck, or chicken feathers will work as well.

Natural Leather Polish

Boil 1¼ cups of linseed oil. Let cool and add 1½ cups of vinegar. Apply with a cloth, then buff.

Washing Windows

I have found newspaper to be the best material I know of, to get sparkling results when cleaning windows. Dip newspaper into white vinegar and wipe the glass until almost dry. Then finish off with a cloth or dry newspaper. Use horizontal strokes when washing outside and vertical strokes when washing inside. This way, if any noticeable streaks show up, you will be able to tell if they are inside or out.

For Hard-to-Reach Areas

Wrap a sock, rag, or sponge around the end of a broom and use to clean behind radiators, ceiling fans, or high corners.

Controlling Odors

During the annual fall and spring cleaning, I find the following mixture simmering on the stove to be a most pleasant air freshener. It seems to facilitate everyone's chores in a most delightful manner.

To a large pot of water, add lemon, apple, and/or orange peelings with sprinkles of cinnamon or cloves. (I once threw in a slice of stale apple pie, which worked quite nicely.)

To absorb smoke odors, place a large oil lamp with a wick inside of a glass jar filled with vinegar or place a large bowl of water in the room.

For unmentionable bathroom odors, strike a match and blow it out after a second or two. The smoke will infiltrate the room.

To absorb the smell of kerosene when using lamp oil, add the juice of 2 limes to 1 gallon of kerosene, stir, and strain through muslin.

To Deodorize a Room

Place a small open cup, half full of vinegar, in the kitchen. It will absorb even the strongest odors (such as Aunt Middle Mary's fish cabbage).

Boiling cinnamon and cloves on the back of the stove

also freshens the air. Baking a whole, unpeeled lemon in the oven with the door slightly ajar, or simmering orange peels for about 15 minutes, also works well.

An open can of coffee grounds has a natural tendency to absorb strong odors.

Dried citrus peel or pinecones thrown on the fire release a pleasant scent.

Sweeping, Dusting, and Mopping

Sweeping, dusting, and mopping are the most important things you can do to prolong the life of your floors, rugs, and furniture. The kitchen should be swept every day. Use a very stiff, tough, corn broom. To toughen the bristles and make it last longer, dip a new broom in hot salt water before using. Allow to dry completely before using.

Begin at the walls and sweep the dirt and dust to the center of the room. Sweep the dust toward you, with repeated, light strokes

A Little Common Sense

Keep a large safety pin near your kitchen sink. Use it to attach rings to your clothes when you wash dishes.

from all four walls, until you have a tidy little pile of dirt in the center of the room. Then, using a whisk broom, sweep the debris into a dustpan, moving it back an inch or so with each sweep until you have collected all the dust. Empty your pan outside in the trash. Sweep all rooms at least once a week—more if you have help. Sweep the rugs as well, and hang them outside and beat the dust and dirt out of them at least two or three times a year. When sweeping rugs and dusting walls, cover the furniture until the particles of dust settle, then uncover and set about dusting.

For dusting furniture, use a clean soft cloth of cotton, or a well-worn dish towel. You will need an ample supply, changing cloths as soon as one becomes soiled, for well and truly, it does no good to just move the dust around the room. Moisten your cloth ever so little, so as to act as a magnet for the dust, but not so wet as to dampen the wood. (Never do that; it will ruin it!) Use gentle circular motions along the grain of the wood with a slight pressure. Fold the cloth as you go so that you have a clean, unused portion of the cloth with each set of strokes. For some of your wood furniture you may wish to use a furniture polishing solution comprised of 1 pint of linseed oil and 1 wineglass of alcohol. Mix well together and apply to furniture with a linen rag. Rub dry with a soft cotton cloth, then polish with a silk cloth.

I have found that my wood floors respond beautifully to hand dusting. This is done in the same manner as dusting furniture. It does require some time and trouble, but the results are well worth it.

The walls also require dusting, preferably at least two times a year. Always dust them before whitewashing, as the wash will not adhere as well to the walls if there is a layer of dust on them. Papered walls do well with a dusting using a barely moist soft cloth.

The kitchen and bathroom floors are best kept clean with sweeping followed by a good mopping. Use the cleaning solution mentioned earlier, but never damp-mop wood floors with it. Rinse and clean your mop after each use, and stand it upside down in the sun to dry and prevent mildew. Never leave a mop damp-side down on the floor. It will ruin the floor and the mop.

When doing your weekly cleaning, always keep the windows open. Ventilating the room is as important to cleaning as anything else you do. The fresh morning air is always best for such purposes.

Miscellaneous Household Tips

☞ Full-strength vinegar applied to a glass will remove the cloudy appearance.

☞ Place a piece of white chalk in your silver chest or jewelry box to absorb moisture and help prevent tarnishing of silverware and jewelry.

☞ Clean tarnished copper with a solution made of equal parts flour, white vinegar, and salt. Rub on, and then wash off in hot water.

☞ Before you hand wash china, crystal, or other delicate items, place a thick towel in the bottom of the sink to cushion them and prevent them from chipping or breaking.

☞ To loosen two drinking glasses that are stuck together, fill the inner glass with cold water and stand them in hot water. Expansion and contraction from the temperature difference will free them.

☞ Remove the rust from knives and other cooking utensils by sticking them in an onion for a day or so. Move them back and forth periodically to get the onion juices going.

☞ To make your own waterproof matches, dip just the tips into melted wax. Apply a thin coating and allow to dry on a piece of waxed paper. Store in a tin or other waterproof container.

☞ Use a dry bar of soap on creaky doors or stuck drawers.

☞ For a sink that drips and keeps you awake at night: Tie a piece of string to the faucet, placing the end down the drain. When the water drips, it will flow down the length of the string, which will absorb enough to silence the maddening drip.

☞ Plain old cold tea will clean woodwork.

☞ Rub a few drops of vanilla extract on your radiators or outer edge of a cast-iron stove. When warmed, the pleasant scent is released.

☞ Stuff wet shoes with newspaper to speed up the drying process.

☞ Put sugar cubes in your empty suitcase to absorb odors.

☞ Tie a dozen pieces of chalk together and hang them in a damp closet. The chalk will absorb the moisture in the air.

☞ A dab of furniture polish in the bottom of your ashtrays will make cleaning easier.

☞ Shoe boxes create ideal storage for photographs, letters, or other personal items. Paint or cover with paper or fabric.

The Care of Beds: The Bedroom

Perhaps no other room (save the kitchen) can better nurture and replenish peace to your loved ones' souls than the bedroom. Shakespeare said it best:

Sleep that knits up the raveled sleeve of care.
The death of each day's life,
sore labor's bath, balm of hurt minds,
great nature's second course,
chief nourisher in life's feast.

Bedrooms are the most private of rooms, and their colors and furnishings should reflect the personal tastes of their occupants. Some of my favorites for the bedrooms are iron or brass beds canopied with lace draperies to give a cozy feel. Linen sheets scented with lavender and cotton quilts provide a restful night's sleep. Bureaus topped off with fresh flowers from the garden and a few of my favorite photographs are pretty to look at each day. A table or desk for writing or meal trays is also useful, along with an easy chair or rocker and an armoire for storing personal items.

The bedroom should be restorative and thoroughly comfortable. To achieve this, thoughtful attention from the housekeeper is all that is needed. Nothing does the housekeeper more credit than clean, smooth, fresh-smelling bedsheets.

Train your family to throw back the bedclothes when they get out of bed, to put away their own clothes, and to open the window and close the door when they leave their rooms in the morning. Your bedroom straightening will be greatly lightened. For by the time you arrive to put the room in order, the bed will be freshly

"Bed is a bundle of paradoxes: we go to it with reluctance, yet we quit it with regret."

—CHARLES CALEB COLTON

aired and ready to be made up, and you won't need to spend time picking up and putting away personal items within the room.

Mrs. Dunwoody's Secret to Dressing the Bed

The secret is clean, fresh sheets, and a tightly made bed with all wrinkles smoothed out. A freshly made, tight bed is a welcome to guests at the end of a long day. *Always* put fresh sheets on the bed for your guests *the day of their arrival.* When sleeping away from home, we become more aware of the smells around us, so you don't want your beds to be anything but fresh and clean.

A well-made bed is infinitely more pleasant than an ill-kept one. Wrinkles and folds are unsightly and uncomfortable. Begin with the bottom sheet, spreading it out, with the center fold following the center of the mattress. This leaves equal amounts hanging on both sides. Tuck the sheet in the top (head) and bottom (foot). Then make a "mitered" corner. (See the diagram on page 37.) Miter the bottom corners of the bottom sheet, then pull it taut and miter its top corners. This smoothes and anchors the whole

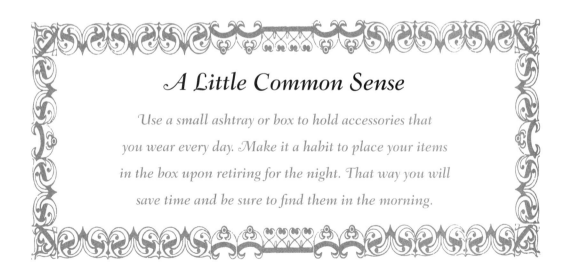

A Little Common Sense

Use a small ashtray or box to hold accessories that you wear every day. Make it a habit to place your items in the box upon retiring for the night. That way you will save time and be sure to find them in the morning.

sheet. Spread the top sheet so that on turnback, the hem will be right-side up. Tuck well at the foot. If the sheet length allows, make a 3-inch fold all the way across, 8 to 12 inches from the foot of the bed, depending on the sleeper's height. This gives plenty of toe room. Tuck in the sheet and miter at the foot only. Miter the blankets at the foot only. The well-mitered top blanket will hold the bed fast. Turn the top sheet back over the blanket and tuck the sides under. Put on the spread, making sure the sides are even. Turn back about 10 inches from the top of the bed. Fluff up each pillow lightly; hold it lengthwise by the corners, and take up the slack in a 1-inch fold. This makes it firmer and neater. Put the pillows at the head of the bed, overlapping the fold of the spread. Pull the spread over the pillows, easing the crease under them and tucking it in at the back. Stand back and admire your work, for you have made a perfect bed!

How to Miter a Corner a Sheet

1. Take a corner of the sheet between your thumb and finger and draw around the corner of the mattress.

2. At the same time, slip your other hand under the side edge of the sheet and draw upward into a diagonal fold.

3. Lay this fold up over the mattress.

4. Now turn under the mattress the part of the sheet which is left hanging.

5. Drop the upper fold and tuck it in under the mattress. This makes a box like a corner. A mitered corner will hold the bedding firmly.

6. All four corners of the lower sheet, if they're long enough, are mitered alike—but do only the bottom corners of the top sheet and covers.

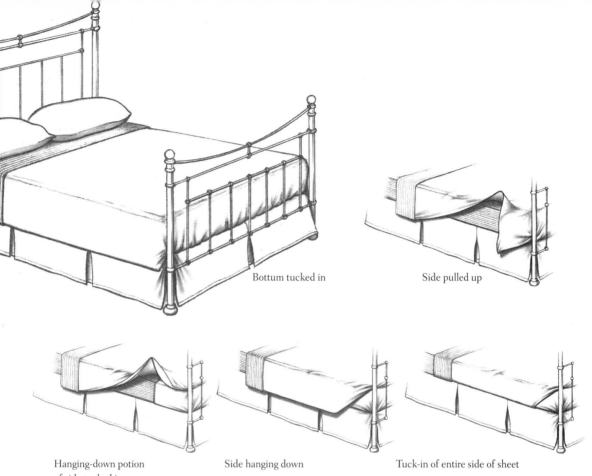

Bottum tucked in

Side pulled up

Hanging-down potion
of side tucked in

Side hanging down

Tuck-in of entire side of sheet

The Guest Room

A room "to be looked at" is what a guest room is *not*. True perfection is the result of nothing more difficult than painstaking attention to detail. Every hostess is obliged to spend twenty-four hours in each room set apart for visitors, for truly a guest sees more in an hour than a host sees in a year. She should sleep in the bed and determine if it is comfortable, and that the sheets are the proper fit. She must also see that the pillows and blankets are adequate and,

Take the time to learn and cater to frequent guests' preferences and habits. Make notes of these things, as well as their favorite foods, so that you may surprise and delight them on their return.

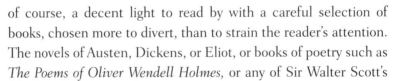

of course, a decent light to read by with a careful selection of books, chosen more to divert, than to strain the reader's attention. The novels of Austen, Dickens, or Eliot, or books of poetry such as *The Poems of Oliver Wendell Holmes,* or any of Sir Walter Scott's entertaining tales would be enjoyable selections. Current magazines and newspapers are also good. Of course, a reliable clock and a mirror are necessary. A comfortable chair and a writing desk with pen and blotter are good too, if possible. There should also be a sturdy candle and a box of matches. A small bedroom will seem larger if you keep the bedspread the same color as the walls.

I find that visits always give pleasure, if not the arrival—the departure. For truly, as Judge Dunwoody used to remark, "Some people stay longer in an hour than others do in a month!"

When we find ourselves a guest in another's home, we must take care to remember Ben Franklin's wise words—"After three days men grow weary of a winch, a guest, and weather rainy." A guest strikes a nail in the wall if he stays but one night. Be careful not to wear out your welcome by mistaking endurance for hospitality. Even best friends must part *sometime.* Leave before your hostess wants you to go. That way you will always be a welcomed sight upon your return.

To Cleanse Feather Beds

To cleanse feather beds without emptying them, on a hot, clear summer day, lay the bed upon a scaffold; wash it well with soap-suds upon both sides, rubbing it hard with a stiff brush. Pour several gallons of hot water upon the bed slowly, and let it drip through. Rinse with clear water; remove it to a dry part of the scaffold to dry; beat and turn it two or three times during the day. Sun until perfectly dry.

Or the feathers may be emptied into barrels, washed in soap-suds, and rinsed; then spread in an unoccupied room and dried, or put in bags made of thin sleazy cloth, and kept in the sun until dry. This kind of work should only be attempted in the long, hot days of June or July. The quality of feathers can be much improved by attention of this kind.

Storing Linens

Tablecloths, towels, and napkins should be kept faultlessly white; tablecloths and napkins starched. After using a tablecloth, lay it in the same folds and put it in a closed place where dust will not reach it. After use, wash items thoroughly and carefully. Never defer attention to such things until they are needed.

All items should be folded as little as possible, but of course this depends on the space available for storage. In general, fold pieces lengthwise in the direction of the warp or grain and then very lightly crosswise until a convenient size is reached. Table-cloths and sheets should be hung on the clothesline or rack until

Stocking the Linen Closet

*At the Dunwoody House we have found this to be the least
amount you should have on hand. As you can afford to, buy more.*

Bathrooms

2 washcloths per person

4 hand towels per person

4 bath towels per person

2 bath mats per bathroom

Bedrooms

2 sets of sheets for each bed

2 pairs of pillowcases for each bed

2 blankets for each bed

1 quilt for each bed

2 bedspreads for each bed

2 mattress pads for each bed

Dining Room

2 tablecloths for everyday use

1 tablecloth for company

12 cloth napkins

Kitchen

6 hand towels

6 dish towels

6 lint-free cloths for
    wiping glassware

thoroughly dry before being folded crosswise. Do not iron in the crosswise folds. Ideally, one lengthwise fold can be made and the tablecloth then rolled on a short pole or roll of paper. Centerpieces and tray cloths should always be rolled.

Dinner napkins are folded into squares. Two folds each way are customary. These are so arranged, that when the napkin is placed on the table at the left of the plate with its edge and selvage parallel to the silver and table edge, any monogram or embroidered figure is on the outside fold. Luncheon napkins also may be folded square, following the same method, but with only one fold each way.

Towels and pillowcases are folded lengthwise into thirds, the center being left on the outside. The one crosswise fold is not ironed in. Handkerchiefs are often folded into a very small square. A better method is to make one fold each way in a woman's hand-kerchief and two folds each way in a man's handkerchief. In the woman's one more fold gives an oblong shape that some people prefer. Store unwrapped soap in the linen closet to scent the linens nicely; this also helps the soap to harden, which makes it long lasting.

To Deter Unwanted Guests

Cockroach Chasers

Mix 4 tablespoons of borax or boric acid, 2 tablespoons of flour, and 1 tablespoon of cocoa powder. Set out in open containers in the kitchen away from children and pets. For a simpler solution, sprinkle borax in cockroach paths. Cockroaches, unlike some of the people who have them, are very clean; as they preen themselves, they will ingest any boric acid that is sticking to them. The boric acid poisons them and scratches and damages their exoskeletons. Boric acid will not harm people or pets unless they ingest a great deal of it. For further prevention in the kitchen, you may find it helpful to mop the floor and wipe down the walls with a solution of water and borax.

The cucumber is an effective cockroach chaser. Place cucumber skins wherever you have a problem. The vegetable has a naturally occurring repellent that cockroaches avoid.

Another method that works well here in the South, before guests arrive dampen a small rug, cloth, or rag and place it on the floor overnight. The bugs will congregate under the cloth and can be destroyed and disposed of in the morning.

Young Charles found that mixing ½ cup of baking soda with 1 tablespoon of powdered sugar causes cockroaches to explode. I have never tested this method, and I am not altogether sure that this would be a good thing.

"Guests of guests cannot bring guests."

Get Rid of Ants

To deter ants, make sure your kitchen shelves are wiped down well, free from any food remains. Wash the shelves with salt and water. Mint tea, citrus juice, salt, ground cinnamon, and boric acid are all good for repelling ants. Sprinkle salt in their paths. Or make a mixture of ⅔ cup of water, ⅓ cup of white vinegar, and 2 to 3 tablespoons of dish soap. Apply where ants are marching. To destroy an ant nest, mix 1 part of confectioners' sugar with 1 part of laundry borax. Sprinkle the mixture over a piece of wood near the nest. The sugar will attract the ants, and the borax will poison them.

To Forestall Bedbugs

"Don't let the bedbugs bite."

*For bedbugs, nothing is so good as the white of eggs
and quicksilver. Add a thimbleful of quicksilver to the white
of each egg; beat until well mixed; apply with a
feather to the bedclothes upon rising.*

Natural Mosquito Repellent

*Dab lavender oil on your pulse points: It repels insects.
Splashing plain rubbing alcohol on yourself and allowing
it to dry will deter mosquitoes from biting you.*

The Rat's Last Supper

*Mix equal amounts of powdered cement and flour. Set next
to pan of water. (Note: This meal usually does not
appeal to dogs and cats.)*

To Prevent Flies from Settling
upon Picture Frames

*Brush them over with water in which onions have been
boiled. (I would advise you to weigh carefully which is more
unpleasant, the number of flies or the smell of the onions,
and proceed accordingly.)*

To Deter Moths

Cloth sachets of lavender will keep moths away from stored clothes and bed linens. Hang small bags of lavender in your closets and tuck them into other stored places.

Mice Control

Stop up any openings to the house or garage with steel wool. Mice will not chew through it. Sprinkle ground cayenne pepper around entry holes. Pests don't care for the smell of it. Mice hate the scent of peppermint extract. Simply sprinkle "pure" peppermint extract on the items in the garage or shed that you don't want mice in or on.

Memorize this old saying for remembering which way to turn a screw: "Lefty Loosey, Rightly Tightly."

A Little Common Sense

Regardless of how tired you are, resist the urge to leave your dishes dirty in the kitchen overnight. There is nothing more depressing for a homekeeper than waking up to a dirty kitchen.

Candles

☞ Chill candles for several hours before lighting; it will cause fewer drips.

☞ You should store at least three candles per day, or twenty-one per week. Fat ones, of course, burn more slowly than thin ones.

☞ Candle wicking can be made with household white string. Soak this in a solution of 6 tablespoons of salt, 6 tablespoons of boric acid, and 3 cups of water for twelve hours. Allow to dry completely, then braid two or three strands to form the wick. To stiffen a candle wick, dip it in melted paraffin wax.

☞ Instant candles: In emergencies you can make an instant candle out of string with one end lying in some cooking oil (or any type of fat—even baking grease) in a dish and the other end hanging over the edge and burning. You get more light if you use six or more strings. They're very smoky, but sometimes that inconvenience is of little consequence.

☞ To remove the smell of smoke from a room, fill a glass jar with vinegar and place a large oil lamp wick inside the jar. It will absorb the lingering odors.

The Care of Books

Books are among the most prized possessions in my home. Proper care of them is imperative. Well-kept books give years of pleasure. As John Milton said, "A good book is the precious lifeblood of a master spirit."

When reading, mark your place with a bookmark or ribbon instead of turning the corner of the page back. To keep your books in good condition, you must remove the dust frequently. To give your books a thorough cleaning, wipe each book with a soft clean cloth and open it, fanning through the pages to toss out the dust. Keep the books dry!

I have found this to be an enjoyable activity, if done together as a family, after dinner one night, or with friends. An interesting discussion always ensues about the books themselves and before you know it, you're done!

Minimize humidity by keeping books in dry places. If your books smell a little musty, place the book in a bag with some bak-

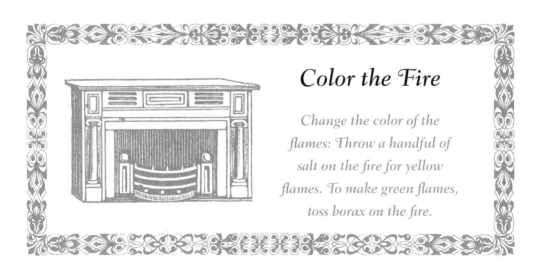

Color the Fire

Change the color of the flames: Throw a handful of salt on the fire for yellow flames. To make green flames, toss borax on the fire.

A Little Common Sense

Every home should be aired out often. Throw open all the windows in the house on cleaning day.

ing soda. Shake and seal and leave overnight. Remove the book and wipe off the soda. Or place them outdoors in the sun and frequently fan out the pages so that the fresh air can reach them. Brush off any mildew or mold. If the pages are damp, sprinkle cornstarch between them and brush it off after a few hours. An afternoon on the front porch, on a dry, hot sunny day, works well, too.

To prevent mildew smells, place a few drops of lavender oil on the book in an inconspicuous spot, such as the inside of the cover, or on a flyleaf. (Staining may occur.) It will also keep the pages smelling fresh. *Caution:* A little lavender oil goes a long way; do not overuse! A little oil of cloves on wooden bookshelves can also help stop mildew from developing. Rub the oil into the shelves thoroughly so that it does not soak into the books.

If you have a damp room and want to keep your books from

smelling mildewed, put an electric lamp on the bookcase and keep it on at all times. (Low wattage will work.)

Group your books into categories. You may arrange them alphabetically by the authors' last name, or by subject matter, or fiction and nonfiction. I enjoy having a special case where only my favorites are allowed.

Fond Records and Keepsakes

Always write names and dates on the backs of pictures. Resist the urge to neglect this duty, thinking "everyone knows who this is." Future generations will not. (Indeed, during my own generation, my memory of names and dates has failed me miserably.)

Save the negatives from your photographs in an envelope marked with the subject matter and date. Consider storing the negatives of your favorite pictures in a safety deposit box. That way, if there is ever a fire or a flood, your photographs will be preserved.

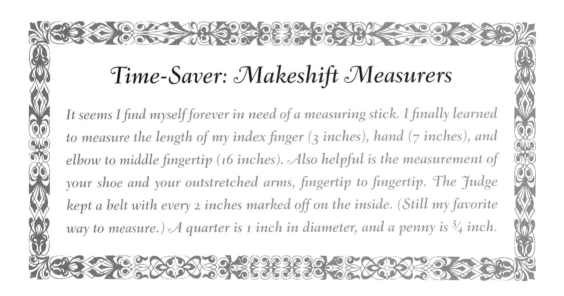

Time-Saver: Makeshift Measurers

It seems I find myself forever in need of a measuring stick. I finally learned to measure the length of my index finger (3 inches), hand (7 inches), and elbow to middle fingertip (16 inches). Also helpful is the measurement of your shoe and your outstretched arms, fingertip to fingertip. The Judge kept a belt with every 2 inches marked off on the inside. (Still my favorite way to measure.) A quarter is 1 inch in diameter, and a penny is ¾ inch.

Write these things down for your children:

Grandparents' full names (include maiden names), date, and place of births (both sets):

_____

_____

Grandfathers' occupations:

_____

Mother and father's full name, date, and place of birth:

_____

_____

How you met:

_____

_____

When you met:

_____

_____

Date married:

_____

Date of deaths:

_____

The family Bible is a good place for such records.*

It is important to preserve and pass on your heritage to your children.

*EDITOR'S NOTE: *Appendix A in the back of this book is another good spot.*

Chapter Three

Miss Sallie Anne's Splendid Directions for Laundry

"*Washing the laundry is what a woman does that nobody notices unless she hasn't done it.*"

—Aunt Middle Mary

Laundry Day

Monday, of course, is laundry day. It is my wish for you, precious children, that you will be blessed with an indispensable helper

such as Miss Sallie Anne to assist you in your laundry duties, but just in case you are not, I have written the following instructions for your reference.

The first step is to gather and sort. As I do this, I always check for torn places which may be made larger by washing. Always mend *before* you wash. Turn all garments inside out. Place the cotton and linens together and the silk and the wools in separate piles. Separate the white from the colored in each pile, and also, sort the very dirty from the slightly soiled. A convenient division of clothes and order of washing is as follows:

1. Cotton and linen: table linen, doilies, centerpieces.

2. Bed linen, dresser scarves, towels.

3. Thin white clothing.

4. Heavy white clothing.

5. Handkerchiefs.

6. Slightly soiled, light-colored garments.

7. Slightly soiled, dark-colored garments.

8. Very dirty garments.

9. Hosiery.

10. Silks.

Before dispatch to the laundry, whether domestic or commercial, an accurate record of the articles sent is essential. I have instructed the housekeeper to record the laundry list in a "washing tally."

A Good Simple Stain Remover

Sponging stains with peroxide will remove many simple stains. Peroxide will not injure wool or silk and is not dangerous to use. It may, however, affect the color of the material, so test on the fabric first.

A Good Washing Mixture

Mix 1 gallon of water, 1 pound of sal soda, and 1 pound of soap; boil for 1 hour, then add 1 tablespoon of spirits of turpentine. Soak the clothes overnight; the next morning, soap them well with the mixture. Boil well for 1 hour; rinse in three waters; add a little bluing to the last water.

Laundry List
for Family of Four
and Two Servants

A Fortnight's Wash, Circa 1880

20 pairs colored wool stockings

20 neck cloths and collars

8 nightcaps

5 cambric gowns

6 flannel petticoats

5 (colored) calico gowns

30 shifts

8 pinafores

2 cotton nightcaps

4 pairs drawers

12 table napkins

4 breakfast tablecloths

4 pillow cases, fine

2 kitchen tablecloths

6 dusters

4 knife cloths

3 pairs common sheets

7 silk handkerchiefs

20 white cotton handkerchiefs

4 frilled collars and tuckers

2 muslins

2 pairs white woolen stockings

2 flannel waistcoats

26 pairs cotton stockings

2 coats

2 pairs trousers

10 white shirts

4 fine tablecloths

4 tray cloths

2 pairs fitted sheets

20 towels

6 glass and 8 kitchen cloths

4 kitchen hand cloths

3 coarse pillowcases

Cleaning Blankets, Woolens, and Flannels

Put 2 heaping tablespoons of borax and 1 pint of soft soap into a large tub of cold water. Make sure all is dissolved before putting in blankets. Let the blankets soak in the water for about 9 hours. Next, rub and rinse, but do not wring out—it will ruin your goods! Hang in the sunshine to dry.

Mildew

Make sure you have no wet or damp articles in the hamper or laundry basket. The items next to them will mildew. Mold thrives in the damp and dark. For stains, try rubbing the article with white vinegar and lemon juice. Saturate the stain. Sprinkle a good bit of salt on the area and scrub in. Place in the sun to dry. (Sunshine is an excellent bleach.) This may need a few treatments, but it does work. Eventually the mildew will come out, but you must be patient.

Coffee Stains

Mix the yolk of an egg with a little warm water. Rub on the stain with a sponge. For stains that have been set in, add a few drops of rubbing alcohol to the egg and water.

Remove Candle Wax from Table Linen

Apply ice to the wax until it freezes (or the cloth may be left out in a dry area overnight during the cold winter months). In this manner, chip off all the frozen wax you

can. Next, lay brown paper over the wax and press with a medium-hot iron. Move the paper as it absorbs the wax, taking care not to redeposit the wax in another area of the cloth. Have patience and continue as long as any wax shows up on the brown paper.

Ink Stains

Try a sponge soaked with milk and rub on the ink spot. This, like mildew stain removal, takes several tries and patience, but it works.

Bloodstains

Wash in warm water until the stain disappears. Use a few drops of ammonia in the water if the stain is resistant. Do not use hot water, as that will set the stain. On heavy items, such as blankets and coats, use a paste of raw starch and warm water. Spread on the stain and, as soon as it's discolored, remove the paste.

Ring around the Collar

Apply a paste of vinegar and baking soda and let set for a quarter to a half hour. Then wash as usual.

Grass Stains

Wash a fresh stain with cold water. Alcohol will dissolve the green color of the grass when the material can't be

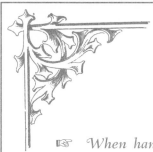

Laundry Tips

☞ When hanging out clothes in the wintertime, wet your hands with vinegar and rub it in before going outside. Be sure they are dry before venturing out. This will prevent your hands from chapping.

☞ Putting cornstarch on your hands and rubbing in will help prevent your skin from splitting in the cold, dry air.

☞ Soak colored cottons overnight in strong salt water and they will not fade.

☞ Always hang slacks or any type of trousers by the legs after washing. The wet weight of the garment will take out almost all of the wrinkles.

☞ White shoe polish will apply more evenly if you rub the shoes with a raw potato or rubbing alcohol before polishing.

☞ Vinegar and water will remove salt stains from shoes and boots.

☞ To whiten laces, wash them in sour milk.

☞ Boil dingy whites (such as underwear or socks) in a pan with lemon slices. The lemon is a natural bleach.

☞ Save old cotton and linen rags in bags for spring cleaning and dusting.

washed. *Moisten with a small amount of kerosene, let stand for a short time, then wash with soap and water.*

For Extra-Dirty Work Clothes

———

Try adding ½ cup of ammonia to the wash. Clothes will come out extra clean.

To Restore Leather and Suede

———

A piece of stale bread will remove fresh spots on leather and suede. Just rub the spots with the bread.

Patent Leather

———

To clean patent leather, first wipe with a wet sponge and then rub with a dry cloth. Next, dip a piece of flannel cloth in olive oil. Rub the leather until it shines. Never let regular shoe polish get on patent leather. It will permanently ruin the patina.

Starching

Starching is an effort to replace the original finish which the textile manufacturer gave to the fabric, and which, in most cases, is removed when the garment is washed. Miss Sallie Anne's recipe for starch gives clothes a beautiful finish, leaving the fabric smooth

Miss Sallie Anne's Secret for Restoring Whiteness to Scorched Linen

Mix 1 cup of vinegar, 2 ounces of fuller's earth, 1 ounce of dried fowl's dung, ½ ounce of soap, and the juice of 2 large onions. Boil all of these ingredients together to the consistency of paste; spread the composition quickly over the damaged part. If the threads have not been actually consumed, after the paste has been allowed to dry on, and the place has subsequently been washed once or twice, every trace of scorching will disappear. (Or, if not, Miss Sallie Anne reports that you won't much care after digging up that fowl's dung and mixing it with onion juice.)

and pliable and giving it a certain "feel" which makes it attractive. There is nothing quite like the feeling of putting on a freshly laundered and starched garment that Miss Sallie Anne has tended to.

Miss Sallie Anne's Superior Recipe for Starch

2–6 tablespoons cornstarch
⅓ cup cold water
1 quart boiling water
½ teaspoon lard, paraffin, or any white wax

———

Mix the starch and part of the cold water, and stir into the boiling water in a double boiler. Use the remaining water

Wash Day

"They that wash on
Monday
Have all the week to dry;
They that wash on Tuesday
Are not so much awry;
They that wash on
Wednesday
Are not so much to blame;
They that wash on
Thursday
Wash for shame;
They that wash on Friday
Wash in need;
And they that wash on
Saturday,
Oh! they're sluts indeed."

—ROBERT HUNT

to rinse out the adhering starch. Add the lard or white wax, and cook for 15 to 20 minutes. Strain if lumps are found. This paste can be thinned with hot water until it gives the stiffness desired for the fabric.

For white clothes, use the starch as hot as the hands can stand. Hot starch penetrates better and more evenly, and does not leave glazed spots when ironed. Keep the bulk of the starch hot and use only a part of it at a time, replacing it frequently when it becomes cold and thin. More satisfactory results are obtained by having two pans of starch, besides the reserve supply. Dilute one with enough water to make a good paste for the thinner garments, and keep the starch in the other pan sufficiently thick for the heavier fabrics.

Starch first those garments which are to be stiffest. Garments wrung very dry before starching will be stiffer than wetter ones.

Ironing

With starched clothes, the iron must be hot enough to glaze the starch; otherwise it will stick and discolor the fabric.

Remove excess starch by sprinkling salt on newspaper and running the iron over it several times. If a pressed article is not completely dry, hang it over a rack to dry out before storing it away.

The ironing board should be well padded, in good light, with a clothes rack or hook handy for ironed pieces.

Slow, unhurried, well-directed motions give best results with hand ironing. Ironing can actually be a ritual of contemplation time if viewed as a time of mental rest rather than a chore. (I have had some of my most creative and inspiring thoughts while ironing.) And it is satisfying to see the efforts of your labor when you hang your family's neatly pressed laundry in its proper place!

Iron with the thread of the goods and until each part is thoroughly dry. Otherwise it will have a puckered appearance. Iron first those parts of the garment that will hang off the board while the rest is being ironed. For example, when ironing a shirt, iron the cuff and the sleeves first, then the collar, and then the body of the shirt starting at one end and continuing around to the other. After ironing a garment, look it over carefully and press again where needed. Gloss on hems, tucks, and seams can be removed by moistening the fabric and exposing it to strong sunlight.

Iron clothes on the right side, except when it is desired especially to bring out the pattern of the fabric. Embroidery appears best when ironed on the wrong side on a thick, soft pad. Cotton-lace dresses often look best when ironed dry on the wrong side. Slip a bit of cardboard into ties before ironing. That way the impression of the seam will not show through on the front.

Fold large items such as a tablecloth in half and iron one side. Then fold in half again (ironed sides together) and iron the other two sides. This is a great time-saver.

To "iron" a hair ribbon in a hurry, grasp both ends and pull the ribbon back and forth against a teakettle that has just been used to boil water.

When you must press something but have no iron, place the

item *carefully* under your mattress overnight. The weight of your body should give it a thorough pressing.

Sewing and Mending Tips

Every home should have a sewing basket. Choose a good-size one, but not so big that you can't carry it from room to room as needed. Inside your basket you will need the following basic supplies:

☞ Sewing needles (assorted sizes).

☞ Thread (light and dark colors, and varying strengths).

☞ A very sharp pair of scissors.

☞ Straight pins kept in a pincushion.

☞ Assorted buttons.

☞ Assorted snaps, hooks, and eyes.

☞ A thimble.

☞ A magnifying glass.

☞ A tape measure.

☞ A seam ripper.

☞ A needle threader.

☞ Safety pins.

☞ Dressmaker chalk.

You will find much satisfaction in being able to repair a fallen button or torn hem, or patching a small hole in a garment. With minimal skill, you can tend to these things as they occur and save yourself quite some expense.

Basic Hand Stitching

Choose a thread color that most closely matches your garment. When in doubt, use black for dark colors or patterns and white for everything else. Do not use a thread longer than you need. A thread the length of your arm or slightly less is usually sufficient. Select a needle sturdy enough for the thickness of the garment you are sewing and thread your needle. Then secure the thread so that it will not pull out of the garment as you are sewing. The easiest way to do this is to tie a knot in the end; or you can make two or three tiny stitches at the beginning and end of your sewing. For greater strength, double your thread and knot it at the end. However, if you are sewing a hem and want the stitching to be less noticeable, knot only one of the loose ends of the thread, leaving the other one hanging down 2 or 3 inches. You must be careful when sewing this way, not to accidentally catch the loose end up in your stitching and begin sewing with a double thread.

Here are examples of the basic sewing stitches:

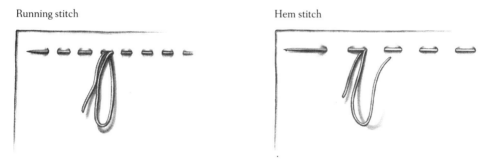

Running stitch

Hem stitch

Helpful Sewing Hints

☞ Stuff your pincushion with your own hair. The oil present in your hair keeps the needles from rusting.

☞ Need a pincushion in a hurry? Use a bar of soap.

☞ Drop a lot of needles when you are sewing and can't seem to find them? Keep a child's magnet in your sewing basket.

☞ Have problems with buttons coming off? On buttons that have four holes, sew only two holes on at a time. Break the thread and knot. Then do the other two with a new piece of thread and knot. This way, when the button comes loose on one set of stitches, the other will keep it in place. Also, using wax-coated string helps buttons stay put.

☞ Need heavy-duty thread for sewing on buttons, et cetera? Run general-purpose thread through beeswax. It will inhibit twisting or knotting and add strength to the thread.

☞ To avoid tangling and twisting, work with no more than 20 inches of thread extending from the needle. If you should still notice twisting of the thread, hold the fabric up, letting the needle and thread dangle beneath it. Allow the thread to spin and untwist, then pick up the needle and continue with sewing.

☞ To remove a hem crease, sponge the material with white vinegar and press with a warm iron.

☞ Zippers won't stick if you rub them with the edge of a bar of soap.

☞ When you're missing a button in a noticeable spot and cannot find one to match, remove a button from a less visible spot and replace it in the place that shows. Then sew the unmatched button in its place.

☞ To ensure that a button is sewn on in the proper place, use dressmaker chalk to mark the spot.

Chapter Four

Notes and Recipes from the Kitchen

"Without the culinary arts, the crudeness of reality would be unbearable."

—JUDGE DUNWOODY

Mrs. Dunwoody's Best-Kept Secret Recipes

Southern Fried Chicken

1 frying-size chicken, 2–2½ pounds, disjointed
1 cup flour
½ teaspoon each salt and pepper
¼ teaspoon ground ginger
¼ teaspoon garlic powder
fat for frying (⅔ shortening, ⅓ butter)

Rinse and pat the chicken dry. Mix the dry ingredients in a brown paper bag. Shake a few pieces of chicken at a time in the bag; shake off excess flour. Heat about 1 inch of fat in a heavy iron frying pan. When the fat is smoking hot, lay in the chicken, taking care not to crowd the pan. Cover and cook until just golden brown on one side. Turn the chicken; cover the pan and cook until the underside is browned. Remove the cover. Cook until the chicken is now a deep, rich brown on one side; turn and fry until the other side is the same. Reduce the heat and let the chicken fry slowly until it is fork-tender, turning it once or twice. When done, drain on paper and serve at once with gravy.

Fried Chicken Gravy, Cream Style

Pour off all but about 2 tablespoons of fat. Stir in 2 tablespoons of flour, stirring and scraping from the bottom of the

pan to get all the crisp bits. Slowly stir in 2 cups of milk. Cook and stir until thickened; season to taste with salt and pepper. (The secret to making good gravy is taking your time.) If more gravy is desired, add extra flour and milk. Serve hot.

Big Mama's Baked Country Ham

The Judge says it is "as spicy as a woman's tongue, as sweet as her kiss, and as tender as her love."

———

Carefully wash a 10- to 12-pound ham and plunge into a big kettle of water until it is completely covered. Then toss in 1 tablespoon of whole cloves, a stick of cinnamon, 3 cloves of garlic, 1 cup of vinegar, and 1 cup of sugar. Let it remain in the kettle over a very slow fire for 3¼ hours. Stifle every boiling bubble that appears. After turning the heat off, let the ham remain in the hot liquor for 4 hours. Take from the water. Remove the top skin; trim, and pat in the following mixture: 1 cup of brown sugar and 1 tablespoon of dry mustard. Dot whole cloves on the fat. Put in a baking pan. Add ¼ cup of vinegar, ¾ cup of water, and bake in a 350-degree oven for 1 hour. Do not baste until the ham is browned. Fifteen minutes before the ham is removed from the oven, make this sauce:

In a saucepan, mix 1 teaspoon of dry mustard, ¼ teaspoon of powdered cloves, ¼ teaspoon of ground cinnamon, 2 tablespoons of vinegar, and a small glass of apple jelly. Heat over a slow fire (low heat) until the jelly is melted, then put the ham on a platter and pour the hot syrup over it. Carve the ham to the bone, like lamb, and over each slice put a spoonful of sauce. Delicious!

Nature does her best to teach us. The more we overeat, the harder she makes it for us to get to the table.

Turnip Greens with Hog Jowl

1 pound fresh mustard greens
½ pound salt pork or fresh hog or
 ham hock (less if desired)
water to cover
1 pound or more young tender
 turnip tops
spring onions

*"My dears,
there are
two choices
for dinner
tonight:
take it or
leave it!"*

—AUNT MIDDLE
MARY'S RESPONSE TO
THE QUESTION,
"WHAT'S FOR
DINNER?"

Wash and drain the mustard greens; put in a pot with the meat and barely enough water to cover. Cook until the meat is tender. Wash and drain the turnip tops; boil in a separate pot until tender. Add to the meat pot and simmer for a few minutes. Drain, but save the liquid. Arrange the meat over the greens. Cut and sprinkle over several young spring onions. Serve the "pot likker" in cups. Serve with corn bread.

Savannah's Skillet Corn Bread

3 tablespoons bacon grease
2 handfuls white corn meal (1½–2 cups)
1 cup buttermilk
½ teaspoon soda (level)
1 teaspoon salt (level)
1 egg, beaten

Melt the bacon grease in a skillet. Mix the corn meal with the buttermilk, soda, and salt. Add the beaten egg. Pour most of the hot grease melted in the skillet into the bread batter. Pour the mixture back into the skillet and bake in a 375-degree oven for about 25 minutes. Cut into wedges like a pie and serve.

The Carter Sisters' Sunday Picnic Gelled Salad

The guests will be positively giddy!

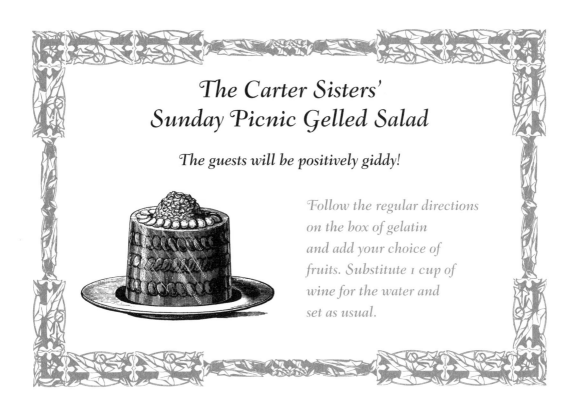

Follow the regular directions on the box of gelatin and add your choice of fruits. Substitute 1 cup of wine for the water and set as usual.

Miss Sallie Anne's Succotash

The perfect complement to any meat.

For a change, Sallie Anne has taught me to cook 1 pint of butter beans or lima beans and 1 pint of sweet corn together, cutting the corn from the cob. Boil the beans with 1 cup of milk or cream and 3 tablespoons of butter, plus salt and pepper to taste. Boil until almost tender before adding the corn. Cook the corn for about 10 minutes. Season with butter, salt, and pepper.

Southern Baking Powder Biscuits

So fluffy they almost float off the plate!

1 cup flour
¼ teaspoon salt
¼ teaspoon sugar
2 teaspoons baking powder
2 rounded tablespoons shortening
milk (about ⅓ cup)

———

Preheat the oven to 400 degrees. Sift together the dry ingredients. Work in the shortening, using your hands. Add enough milk to make a workable soft dough. Knead the dough until smooth. Roll out on a floured surface to the desired thickness and cut with a water glass. Bake biscuits for 15 minutes, or until golden brown and puffy.

Bride's Biscuits

Known to have saved many a marriage!

½ cup butter, softened
3 ounces cream cheese
1 cup flour
spoonful of love

———

Blend together the butter and the cheese. Mix in the flour and knead the mixture with love to make a dough. Roll out on a floured board and cut with a small cutter. Bake in a preheated 350-degree oven until the biscuits are lightly brown and puffy, about 12 to 15 minutes. Serve hot with a kiss.

Ambrosial Pecan Pie

The Judge's favorite!

3 eggs
1 pound light brown sugar
¼ cup butter, melted
pinch of salt
1 teaspoon vanilla
piecrust
1 cup pecans, chopped

Stir the eggs lightly. Beat in slowly the sugar and the melted butter. Add the salt and vanilla. Line a pie plate with pastry and sprinkle half of the pecans over the bottom. Pour the mixture into the unbaked pie shell. Sprinkle the remaining pecans over the top of the mixture. Bake in a 350-degree oven for 40 minutes, or until the pie is almost set. Reduce the heat to 225 degrees and bake for 15 minutes more, or until the pie is thoroughly set.

Mammie Jane's Piecrust

A rich crust.

2¼ cups flour
1 teaspoon salt
1 cup shortening
3 tablespoons water
3 tablespoons lemon juice

Mix the flour, salt, and shortening; blend until it resembles coarse corn meal. Sprinkle the water and lemon juice over, using 1 tablespoon at a time; mix. Roll into a ball and wrap

in waxed paper. Chill. Roll out on a floured board when ready to use.

Makes 3 9-inch shells.

Cut and Come Again Pie

A fitting name!

Line a deep plate, slightly greased, with a good crust. Cut ripe, juicy apples into thin slices; fill the plate, layering alternately apples, a layer of sugar, and then spice. A tumbler of brown sugar will season a quart of apples with a pleasant taste. Use more if they are not yet sweet tasting. Next, grate over half a teaspoon of nutmeg, the same of cinnamon, the same of coriander seed. Add half a tumbler of water; put on the upper crust. Bake for 45 minutes in a medium-hot oven (350 degrees). Watch the crust carefully to avoid over-browning. Serve with rich cream. Simply irresistible!

"No mean woman can cook well, for it calls for a light head, a generous spirit, and a large heart."

—JUDGE DUNWOODY

Mammie's Muffins

Legendary!

Beat separately 3 eggs. Make a smooth batter by mixing 2 cups of flour with the eggs and adding 1 cup of sweet milk, or enough to make a thin batter; butter the size of a hen's egg; salt to taste. Heat the oven or pan in which the muffins are to be baked; grease the rings; place them upon the pan. Dissolve in half a wineglass of warm water, 2 teaspoonfuls of cream of tartar; stir this into the batter, and, just before pouring the batter into the rings, stir in a teaspoon of baking soda. Bake quickly, without blistering. When eaten, they should be torn open. To cut them open with a knife is an offense so grave that the cook will find it difficult to forgive.

Christmas Ginger Cakes

The superior version. I bake this prior to the arrival of company, as it makes the house smell so inviting.

4 eggs
1 cup sugar
1 cup butter
1 pound flour
1 cup sour milk
1 quart molasses with 1 even tablespoon baking soda beaten in
1 cup lard
1 tablespoon ginger

The eggs and sugar should be beaten together as for cake; the butter worked into the flour. Mix together milk, molasses, and ginger, and add to dough as needed. After mixing the ingredients thoroughly, handle as little as possible. Flour your board and rolling pin well, as the dough should be as soft as can be handled. Roll ¼ inch thick; cut with any shaped tin, and bake in a quick oven (400 degrees).

The Hidden Mountain

A very pretty supper dish; this recipe is more than a hundred years old.

6 eggs
a few slices of citron
½ cup cream
sugar to taste
layer of any type of jam

Beat the whites and the yolks of the eggs separately; then mix them, and beat well again, adding a few thin slices of the citron, the cream, and sufficient pounded sugar to sweeten it nicely. When the mixture is well beaten, put it into a buttered pan, and fry the same as a pancake; but it should be three times the thickness of an ordinary pancake. Cover it with jam and garnish with slices of citron and holly leaves. This dish is served cold.

Sufficient for 4 persons (or 2 very hungry ones)

The Children's Favorite Breakfast

Mother's, too! For she utilizes the otherwise wasted bread.

Spread stale bread with butter or marmalade and layer in a baking dish. Mix 2 beaten eggs with 1¼ cups of milk and pour over all. Bake in a moderate oven until lightly brown. Serve with favorite syrup.

A Little Common Sense

Use a knife dipped in boiling water to cut a fresh loaf of bread or to frost a cake. You will love the results!

Dessert for Unexpected Guests

For the hostess in a hurry!

Pan-fry peeled and thickly sliced bananas in butter and brown sugar for 2 minutes or so. Sprinkle with orange juice and a little rum. Powdered sugar also works well. (Note: I find that this dish is most impressive when the simplicity of preparation is not revealed.)

Sherbet

A summertime favorite.

To 6 lemons and 8 sweet oranges, sliced, and the seeds removed, put 1 gallon of water and sweeten to taste. Freeze or use ice.

Miss Lucinda's Lemon Ice Water

Perfect on a hot summer day. Very refreshing!

Rub lumps of sugar upon the rinds of 4 lemons until a pound of loaf sugar is used; pour over it a quart of water, squeezing in the juice. Freeze, or make a lemonade, sweeter than when not intended to freeze, and more highly flavored. Freeze and serve in glasses with a sprig of mint.

Fresh Peach Ice Cream

It disappears immediately!

Pare and stone 1 quart of very soft peaches. Add to them 2 cups of sugar, and mash them thoroughly. When ready to freeze, add 2 quarts of rich cream. Freeze in a hand-turned freezer. When frozen, this will fill a dish holding 4 quarts.

Candied Rose Petals

Simply beautiful!

In a small bowl, slightly beat one egg white. On a plate, sprinkle a good layer of sugar. Dip rose-petal leaves first in egg white and then in sugar so they are coated on both sides. Dry on a rack or screen. Use on candy or cake tray as a garnish, or as a border for a cake plate.

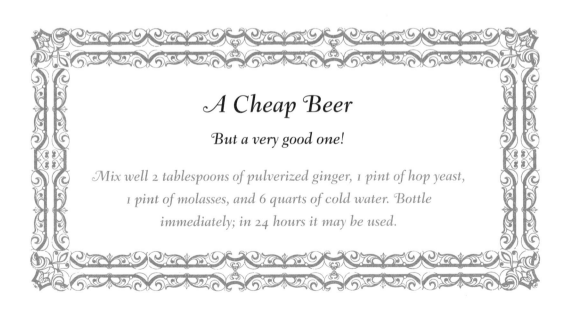

A Cheap Beer

But a very good one!

Mix well 2 tablespoons of pulverized ginger, 1 pint of hop yeast, 1 pint of molasses, and 6 quarts of cold water. Bottle immediately; in 24 hours it may be used.

The Robert E. Lee Cake

The most famous historical cake.

10 egg yolks, beaten
2 cups sugar
1 teaspoon lemon juice
1 teaspoon orange juice
grated rind of 1 lemon
10 egg whites, stiffly beaten
2 cups flour
½ teaspoon salt

———

Beat the egg yolks until lemon colored; add the sugar, fruit juices, and rind. Fold in the stiffly beaten egg whites; last, add the flour sifted with the salt, by sprinkling in the flour gently by the handful. Bake in round ungreased pans, making three medium layers or four very thin ones. Ice with boiled icing (below).

Boiled Icing for the Robert E. Lee Cake

3 cups sugar
1 cup water
3 egg whites, stiffly beaten
1 tablespoon lemon juice
grated rind of 1 orange
grated rind of 1 lemon
1 cup grated coconut

———

Boil the sugar and water until the syrup spins a thread. Pour into the egg whites, stirring constantly. Add the lemon juice and grated orange and lemon rind to the icing.

Spread between the layers and on the top and sides of the cake. Sprinkle the grated coconut all over the top and sides.

Captain Clementine's Mint Julep

A most inviting summer drink.

Put into a tumbler about a dozen sprigs of the tender shoots of mint; upon them put a spoonful of white sugar, and equal proportions of peach and common brandy, so as to fill up one-third; then take rasped or pounded ice and fill up the tumbler. Epicures rub the lips of the tumbler with a piece of fresh pineapple; the tumbler is itself very often encrusted outside with stalactites of ice. "As the ice melts, you drink." Very refreshing!

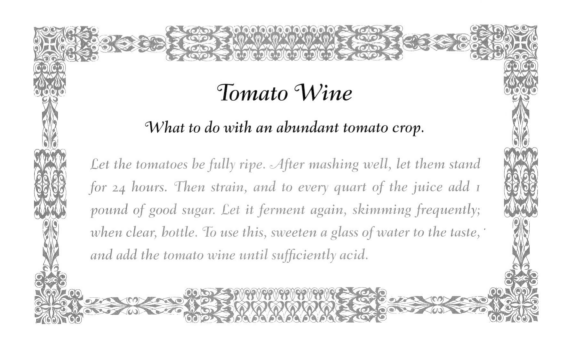

Tomato Wine

What to do with an abundant tomato crop.

Let the tomatoes be fully ripe. After mashing well, let them stand for 24 hours. Then strain, and to every quart of the juice add 1 pound of good sugar. Let it ferment again, skimming frequently; when clear, bottle. To use this, sweeten a glass of water to the taste, and add the tomato wine until sufficiently acid.

Your Favorite Recipes

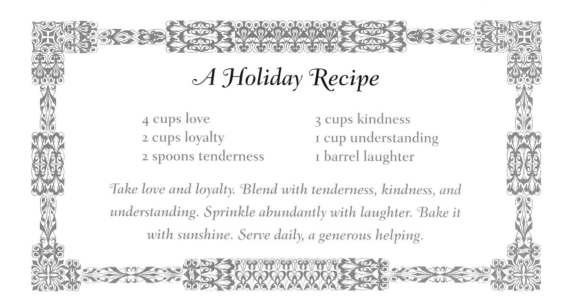

A Holiday Recipe

4 cups love	3 cups kindness
2 cups loyalty	1 cup understanding
2 spoons tenderness	1 barrel laughter

Take love and loyalty. Blend with tenderness, kindness, and understanding. Sprinkle abundantly with laughter. Bake it with sunshine. Serve daily, a generous helping.

Useful Notes from the Kitchen

The kitchen is the engine room of the house. It should be well planned with plenty of work- and storage space, and be pleasant to work in and easy to clean. Efficiency and shortcuts in the kitchen help to keep a woman sane. People are always asking me the secret to this or that. Well, my dear children, I will finally tell you . . . *the secret is common sense.*

For instance:

☞ My two best friends in the kitchen are a chopping board and a set of very sharp knives. The board should be 2 feet by 10 inches and made like a ship's deck so there are no joints or cracks for food to lodge in. I like to use unvarnished wood and treat it by rubbing it with heated raw linseed oil. Let it dry overnight and it will never stain. The knives should be the very best you can afford.

☞ Use wooden spoons for *all* stirring.

☞ When frying, always get your pan hot first, then add your butter or oil. Meat and eggs won't stick.

☞ When dipping meat pieces into egg batter and then crumbs, use your left hand for applying the egg, and your right for the crumbs. Then your fingers won't get gluey.

☞ When greasing pans or molds, use butter for hot dishes, oil for cold (butter stiffens and sticks when chilled, defeating your purpose).

☞ To get rid of that buildup of calcium or lime in your kettle, simply pour in about ¼ cup of vinegar and add about a quart of water. Bring the water to a boil and allow it to boil for 10 or 15 minutes. Empty the pot, wash and rinse thoroughly, and the white deposits will be gone.

Molding Clay for Children

What to do on a rainy day.

Mix well 1 cup of flour, ½ teaspoon of salt, and 2 teaspoons of cream of tartar. Then, in a medium saucepan, add 1 cup of water, 1 teaspoon of oil, and food coloring. Cook over medium heat for 3 minutes or until the mixture pulls from the sides of the pan. Remove from the heat and knead. Let cool before giving to children.

☞ To eliminate odors from cutting boards, rub them with a paste of baking soda and water, then rinse well. For really bad odors, you may want to leave the paste on for a while before rinsing.

☞ A leaf of lettuce dropped into a pot absorbs the grease from the top of the soup. Remove the lettuce and throw it away as soon as it has served its purpose.

☞ To prevent splashing when frying meat, sprinkle a little salt into the pan before putting the fat in.

☞ When bread is baking, a small dish of water in the oven will help to keep the crust from getting hard.

☞ Rinse a pan in cold water before scalding milk to prevent sticking.

☞ Dip the spoon in hot water before measuring butter or shortening. The fat will slip out easier that way.

☞ Use a thread instead of a knife to cut cakes for multilayered recipes. It's easier than cutting with a knife, and you can get wafer-thin layers.

☞ To liven up stale cakes, turn the cake upside down and poke a few holes in it with a slim utensil. Spoon rum or brandy over it and let stand overnight.

☞ Never pour water on flaming oil or fat. It will make the fire spread. If the fire is inside the pan, slap on the lid. If outside, turn off the heat and douse the flames by tossing on a handful of salt or baking soda.

☞ Boil a few slices of lemon in a saucepan to quickly erase unpleasant burned-food smells.

☞ Take extra care in washing surfaces and utensils that come in contact with raw meat.

☞ Wash your hands thoroughly and often.

☞ Heat milk slowly and stir constantly to prevent its separating and forming a skin on top. (But don't ever discard the skin; that's the richest part.)

☞ To keep a block of cheese until grating, dip it in brandy and wrap it well in plastic. Brandy used for preserving and dipping can be saved and used again for these purposes.

☞ A fresh egg will sink in water; a stale one will float.

☞ For light and fluffy scrambled eggs, add a little milk or water while beating the eggs.

☞ When making scrambled eggs for a crowd, I discovered that a pinch of baking powder and 2 teaspoons of water for each egg makes them go a lot farther.

☞ Can't remember if the egg is fresh or hard boiled? Spin it. If it wobbles, it's raw. If it spins easily, it's hard boiled.

☞ For perfect hard-cooked eggs, cover the eggs with cold water and bring to a boil. Then turn off the heat and let the eggs sit on the burner for 10 to 15 minutes.

☞ When cooking with raw eggs, you'll get best results if you chill them first. They separate better and thicken mayonnaise or hollandaise sauce faster.

☞ To test egg whites: If they adhere to the bowl when you turn it upside down, they are well whipped.

☞ When poaching eggs, try water flavored with a little tarragon vinegar for a subtle, different taste.

☞ A no-fail way to separate eggs is to break them one at a time into a small funnel over a cup. The white will pass through into the cup, and the yolk will be left behind in the funnel.

Hints for Herbs and Seasonings

☞ An herb's aromatic oils are strongest in the morning, after a night's rest. So gather the leaves from your garden as early in the day as possible, after the dew has dried, but before the sun gets hot.

☞ Place spare sprigs of fresh herbs directly on the oven rack toward the end of the baking or roasting time. The aroma will stimulate your family's taste buds and welcome arriving guests to the anticipated feast.

☞ Flavor your sugar for baking by adding your favorite scent to it. I store vanilla beans in my sugar jar, but you can also use fruit zest, mint, cinnamon sticks, or other aromatic flavors.

☞ To keep dill, mint, or tarragon fresh, wash and dry well, then strip the sprigs from the stalks and store them in an airtight jar, in a cool place.

☞ Rub dry herbs between your fingers or dehydrate them with a little water to release their fragrance.

☞ When using fresh herbs in a recipe, use three times the amount you would use of dried.

☞ For garlic: Never cook garlic fast; it should always be allowed to cook slowly. Never cook it alone. Chop it in a little salt so

A Little Common Sense

For quick and handy seasoning while cooking
on the stove, keep on hand a large shaker containing
6 parts of salt and 1 part of pepper.

the pieces won't cling to your knife or board. Garlic should be as fresh as your salad greens, or it becomes dry and tasteless. To sweeten garlic-scented fingers, rub them with a raw tomato (which you can cut up and use in your salad).

☞ Dry mustard will remove onion odors from your hands or cutting board. Rub in, then rinse off.

☞ It is important when and how you add salt in cooking. To blend with soups and sauces, put it in early, but add it to meats just before taking them from the stove. In cake ingredients, salt can be mixed in with the eggs. When cooking vegetables, always salt the water in which they are cooked. Put salt in the pan when you fry fish.

☞ Mix 1 cup of finely ground sugar with 1½ tablespoons of cinnamon. Store in large saltshaker and sprinkle on buttered toast.

Secrets for Mouthwatering Sauces

☞ Add sifted flour to melted butter, off the heat, for a smoother mixture. For that matter, when adding any liquid to a sauce base, stir it in off the heat.

☞ Add hot sauce to cold sauce two spoonfuls at a time so the cold warms up gradually and doesn't curdle.

☞ Use a wooden spoon and scrape the bottom to make sure nothing sticks.

☞ The secret to a good sauce is time. Never cook on high heat. Be patient: Stir and cook on low-to-medium heat.

☞ To correct a too-thick sauce, heat until simmering, then beat in, a spoonful at a time, a little cream or stock until the consistency is right.

☞ To correct a too-thin sauce, blend a teaspoon of flour with a teaspoon of soft butter. Stir into the sauce (off the heat) until smooth. Simmer.

☞ To correct a separated sauce, beat in a tablespoon or so of cold water for hollandaise or chocolate; use hot water for mayonnaise.

Hints and Guide to Color When Meat Buying

☞ Beef should be well marbled and very bright red with white fat.

☞ Chicken should have fat as close to white as possible. If the pinfeather holes are close together, the bird is young and tender. Veal should also be as white as possible. Pork should be pink with as little fat as possible. Lamb should be rosy red and not fatty.

☞ To keep raw meat fresh and odorless, rub it with oil or dip it into its own rendered fat or melted butter before cooling. Don't wrap it.

☞ To keep raw fish fillets fresh and odorless, rinse them with fresh lemon juice and water, dry thoroughly, and wrap.

☞ Never pierce meat when browning; the juices will escape. Use tongs. While cooking, don't let the pieces touch each other or they will stew instead of browning. It's better to do just a few at a time rather than crowding them all in at once. Brown red meats quickly, uncovered; poultry, more slowly.

☞ Never carve any sizable piece of meat or poultry right after it comes out of the oven. Wait 20 minutes for roasts, turkeys, and the like; they will be much easier to slice.

☞ Cook your red meats slowly in a low oven for tender results. It's worth the extra time.

☞ An ounce of chocolate can enrich the flavor of spicy meat or game.

☞ Try using coffee instead of water when cooking lamb for stew. Coffee complements the flavor of lamb and makes the meat juices dark, rich, and flavorful.

Market Guide for Buying Fruit and Vegetables

Experience is the best guide when selecting fruits and vegetables for your family, but here are a few pointers:

- *Asparagus.* Stalks should be tender yet firm; tips should be close and compact. Choose stalks with very little white—they are more tender. Use it immediately, because it toughens rapidly.

- *Beans, snap.* Those with small seeds inside the pods are best. Avoid beans with dry-looking pods.

- *Berries.* Select plump, solid berries with good color.

- *Broccoli, brussels sprouts, and cauliflower.* Flower clusters on broccoli and cauliflower should be tight and close together. Brussels sprouts should be firm and compact. Smudgy, dirty spots may indicate insects.

- *Cabbage and head lettuce.* Choose heads heavy for size. Avoid cabbage with worm holes, or lettuce with discoloration or soft rot.

- *Cucumbers.* Choose long slender cucumbers for best quality. They may be dark or medium green, but yellow ones are undesirable.

- *Peas and lima beans.* Select pods that are well filled but not bulging. Avoid dried, spotted, yellowed, or flabby pods.

- *Root vegetables.* Should be smooth and firm. Very large carrots may have woody cores; oversize radishes may be pithy; oversize turnips, beets, and parsnips may be woody. Fresh carrot tops usually mean fresh carrots, but the condition of leaves on most other root vegetables does not indicate degree of freshness.

- *Cantaloupes.* Thick, close netting on the rind indicates best quality. Cantaloupes are ripe when the stem scar is smooth and the space between the netting is yellow or yellow-green. They are best to eat when fully ripe with a pleasant, sweet, fruity odor.

- *Honeydews.* Honeydews are ripe when the rind has a creamy to yellowish color and velvety texture. Immature honeydews are whitish green.

- *Watermelons.* Ripe watermelons have some yellow color on one side. If melons are white or pale green on one side, they are not ripe.

- *Oranges, grapefruit, and lemons.* Choose those heavy for their size. Smoother, thinner skins usually indicate more juice.

Most skin markings do not affect quality. Oranges with a slight greenish tinge may be just as ripe as fully colored ones. Light or greenish yellow lemons are more tart than deep yellow ones. Avoid citrus fruits showing withered, sunken, or soft areas.

- *Pineapples.* Pineapples are ripe when a leaf at the top of the pineapple pulls out easily.

Helpful Hints on Fruits

☞ Ripen green bananas by wrapping them in a wet dish towel and placing in a paper bag.

☞ It is easy to remove the white membrane from oranges—for fancy desserts or salads—by soaking them in boiling water for 5 minutes before you peel them.

☞ You can get more juice from a dried-up lemon or lime if you heat it for 5 minutes in boiling water before you squeeze it.

☞ Dip bananas in lemon juice right after they are peeled. They will not turn dark, and the faint flavor of lemon really adds quite a bit to the taste. The same may be done with apples.

☞ Soak dried fruits such as prunes, bananas, apricots, and figs in a large canning jar filled with brandy. They make wonderful desserts when used in baking.

☞ To ripen green tomatoes, place them in a paper bag with an apple or ripe tomato. Store the bag in a warm dark place for 2 days or until the tomatoes ripen and turn red.

Hints for Cooking Vegetables

☞ Blanching helps to keep firmness, texture, color, and flavor in green beans, carrots, leeks, and celery. After slicing, put the pieces in a pan and cover them with cold water. Bring slowly to a boil, drain, and then cook according to recipe.

☞ When cooking carrots, peas, beets, or corn, add a small amount of sugar to the water to keep the flavor.

☞ Never salt the water you cook corn in. It will toughen the corn.

☞ Store tomatoes with stems pointed down and they will stay fresh longer.

☞ Cut off both ends of cucumbers to avoid bitterness. To bring out their taste, slice them a half hour before using, sprinkle with salt, and keep cool.

☞ To avoid tears, chill onions before slicing, or sprinkle fresh lemon juice on the flat surfaces after you've cut the onions in half.

☞ Never cut salad greens with a knife: It bruises them and makes them bitter. Tear them gently into bite-size pieces, by hand.

☞ The secret to crisp salads is to dry the greens thoroughly after washing. I dry them piece by piece before I tear them. Shiny dressings won't stick to salad greens unless they are dry. The best way to toss them is with your own two hands.

☞ Don't store potatoes near apples because apples give off ethylene gas, which causes potatoes to spoil.

☞ Potatoes soaked in salted water for 20 minutes before baking will bake more rapidly.

☞ Sweet potatoes will not turn dark if put in salted water (5 teaspoons salt to 1 quart of water) immediately after peeling.

☞ Let raw potatoes stand in cold water for at least a half hour before frying to improve the crispness of fried potatoes.

☞ A few drops of lemon juice in the water will whiten boiled potatoes.

☞ If you add a little milk to the water in which cauliflower is cooking, the cauliflower will remain attractively white.

☞ When cooking cabbage, place a small tin cup or can half full of vinegar on the stove near the cabbage, and it will absorb all odor from it.

☞ If you have an overabundance of zucchini from your garden, peel it, chop into small pieces, and liquefy it as much as possible. Strain the "milk" from the zucchini and use it for a milk substitute in breads, puddings, biscuits, meat loaves, and the like. Three medium zucchinis can yield nearly 2 cups of milk.

A Little Common Sense

Keep a pair of kitchen scissors handy for chopping ingredients such as herbs, or for cutting bacon, etc.

Essential Equivalents
for Cooks

120 drops water . . . . .1 teaspoon

60 drops thick fluid . . . . .1 teaspoon

2 teaspoons . . . . .1 dessert spoon

3 teaspoons . . . . .1 tablespoon

4 tablespoons . . . . .¼ cup

5⅓ tablespoons . . . . .⅓ cup

8 tablespoons . . . . .½ cup

10⅔ tablespoons . . . . .⅔ cup

12 tablespoons . . . . .¾ cup

16 tablespoons . . . . .1 cup

1 cup . . . . .8 ounces

½ cup . . . . .1 gill

2 cups . . . . .1 pint

2 pints . . . . .1 quart

4 cups . . . . .1 quart

4 quarts . . . . .1 gallon

8 quarts . . . . .1 peck

4 pecks . . . . .1 bushel

16 ounces . . . . .1 pound

32 ounces . . . . .1 quart

8 ounces liquid . . . . .1 cup

1 ounce liquid . . . . .2 tablespoons

How to Season and Care for a Cast-Iron Skillet

A cast-iron skillet is a *must* for any self-respecting Southern cook!

For a New Cast-Iron Skillet

1. First wash your pan very thoroughly with a mild dishwashing liquid. Rinse and dry completely with a dishcloth. You must never let your cast-iron cookware drain dry; that is inviting rust!

2. Now, grease the inside with lard. Rub the grease in. Lightly grease the outside of the pan also. Wipe away any surplus. Do the same for the lid, if it has one.

3. Place it in a slow oven (250 to 275 degrees) and let it "season" (bake) for 8 to 10 hours, or overnight.

4. Do not put the lid on while treating it—you'd need a crowbar to pry it open again.

5. Let your pan cool naturally. It is now ready for use.

6. You can apply a second coat if you like. Just repeat the procedure. If the first coat is spotty and bare, a second or third application will take care of that. Since there is now no exposed metal, your beans or stews can be left in your cast-iron cookware with no fear of rust or metallic taste.

Your seasoned pans will get sealed "coal black" with use, and that's what they are supposed to do. Don't use cast-iron pans for food high in acid content or at a temperature higher than 350 degrees, or the pan may crack. Don't leave a pan on high heat with no liquid in it. First it will get red hot, and then it will crack in two.

Cleaning Cast Iron

Wash with a dishcloth using very mild soap and water. Don't scrape it with any sharp objects; you may gouge off the coating. Don't use anything that might leave scratches on the surface, as food tends to stick in them. Use salt for scouring. Never let drip dry; always dry with a cloth. If you care for them in this manner, they will last forever. I have Dear Mother's cast-iron Dutch oven and skillets, which are fifty-five years old at this writing.

Quantities to Serve
a Hundred People

To serve fifty people, divide by two; to serve twenty-five people, divide by four.

Coffee. . . . . 3 pounds

Loaf sugar. . . . . 3 pounds

Cream. . . . . 3 quarts

Whipping cream . . . . 4 pints

Milk . . . . 6 gallons

Fruit cocktail . . . . 2½ gallons

Soup . . . . 5 gallons

Oysters . . . . 18 quarts

Meat loaf . . . . 24 pounds

Ham . . . . 40 pounds

Beef . . . . 40 pounds

Roast pork . . . . 40 pounds

Chicken for chicken pie . . . . 40 pounds

Potatoes . . . . 35 pounds

Scalloped potatoes . . . . 5 gallons

Baked beans . . . . 5 gallons

Beets. . . . . 30 pounds

Cauliflower. . . . . 18 pounds

Cabbage for slaw . . . . 20 pounds

Carrots . . . . 33 pounds

Bread . . . . 10 large loaves

Rolls 200

Butter . . . . 3 pounds

Potato salad . . . . 12 quarts

Fruit salad . . . . 20 quarts

Vegetable salad. . . . . 20 quarts

Lettuce . . . . 20 heads

Salad dressing . . . . 3 quarts

Pies 18

Cakes 8

Ice cream . . . . 4 gallons

Cheese . . . . 3 pounds

Olives . . . . 1¾ pounds

Pickles . . . . 2 quarts

Nuts . . . . 3 pounds, sorted

To Determine Cooking Temperature by Hand

Despite the Judge's jokes that I used to do this by placing my hand on the floor of the oven and then screaming out the correct temperature in the moments that followed, this method suffices well and truly, and is remarkably accurate:

Hold your palm close to where the food will be cooking. Count "one-and-one, two-and-two," and so on, for as many seconds as you can hold your hand still.

Seconds Counted	Heat	Temperature
6–8	Slow	250–350°
4–5	Moderate	350–400°
2–3	Hot	400–450°
1 or less	Very Hot	450–500°

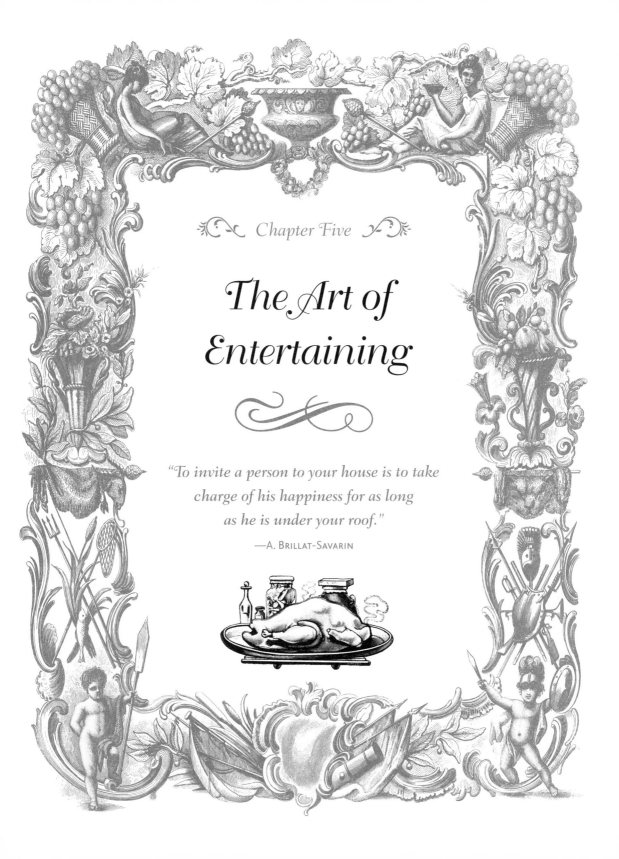

Chapter Five

The Art of Entertaining

"To invite a person to your house is to take charge of his happiness for as long as he is under your roof."

—A. Brillat-Savarin

Mrs. Dunwoody's Essential Guide to Absolutely Delightful Parties

A social life can be one of life's greatest pleasures. Indeed, as I write this, in the eighth decade of life, some of my most amusing and fondest memories are of times in which I entertained friends and family at home. Social life is important not only for the personal satisfaction it brings and the business relationships it fosters, but also because it contributes to your character and growth as a person. Spending time with others helps to build deep and lasting friendships, adds to our knowledge of the world, culture, and hospitality, and keeps our perspective in balance, as we mingle and interact with those who do not necessarily share all of our own opinions.

Children, you will remember when you were young, your father would often invite interesting personalities to dine with us from whom we could all learn some unusual trade, occupation, or school of thought. The Judge often said that one could learn more from five interesting persons than from twenty books. I have to admit he was right, for he certainly taught me more of life than any book could have.

I believe party planning to be a fine art. It is a learned talent which not everyone possesses. But for you, precious children, I shall leave you all of my secrets along with the wish that you will gain as much pleasure from the art as I have.

A *good* hostess can be casual with a hundred guests under her roof. And a furrow of worry indicates to everyone that you're not a smart hostess. The secret of successful entertaining is to never let your guests suspect how much hard work and careful planning went into the party. Genuinely smart hostesses learn from studying the fine art of hospitality and then doing a right sizable amount of work *before* each party. The most common mistake of hostesses is that they do not plan sufficiently far ahead to have the work out of the way, and are therefore tired out and distraught by the time of the party.

When planning a party I begin by establishing the *event, theme, date,* and *time.* Suggestions for parties are of course the usual: birthday, anniversary, engagement, wedding, and showers for expectant mothers along with any of the traditional holidays, such as New Year's Day or Valentine's Day. But other good suggestions include housewarmings, open house, hayrides, sleigh rides, a circus party, a costume party, a grand ball, or even designing an event of your very own. My uncle Jackson and his wife, Olivia, were known for their "Leap Year Celebration" which was held once every four years on February 29. All of the guests knew that each leap year they were to reserve that evening for the lavish soiree. Years later, Aunt Olivia ceased even to mail invitations, so eagerly anticipated and well attended was the event.

Some suggested ways of entertaining include:

- *Breakfast parties.* Sunday noon or 1:00 P.M. Informal, no more than eight guests.

- *Luncheon.* Light simple food, beautifully presented. Usually for ladies only; may precede cards or other games.

- *Tea parties.* Simple and intimate. Light, simple food; may be small or large. Fun to make a mother–daughter theme or to honor a bride before her wedding.

- *At home.* Tea, at home, at the same time each week or month, consistently. Very simple and cheerful.

- *Children's parties.* Usually birthday. (Aunt Middle Mary always used to say the main purpose of giving parties for children is to remind yourself that there are children more awful than your own.)

- *Cocktail parties.* An easy, comparatively inexpensive way of entertaining a large crowd since you are not expected to feed your guests a meal. Usually 5:00 to 7:00 P.M. May precede a larger, more formal event or gathering.

  - *Dinner parties.* Best when done elaborately. An inexpensive menu may be selected, but the utmost care and attention should be given to quality and preparation of food. Presentation is paramount. Attention to detail ensures success. For general conversation, party is usually limited to six to ten guests.

- *Buffet suppers.* Requires maximum service for a large group, but can actually be less expensive than a dinner party. Extra helping hands are a must to ensure that each guest is well attended to. The menu may include a choice of two main dishes. Provide adequate means and places for eating.

- *Parties in the evening.* For entertaining large groups, these can be very versatile: large or small, casual or formal. The menu may consist of a variety of food, such as sandwiches, tea, cocktails, or cake. Games may be arranged for the guests' amusement or entertainment.

- *The men's evening.* Provide ample food, drinks, smokes, ashtrays, card tables, et cetera. The hostess and her children should be inconspicuous.

- *Outdoor parties.* Wonderful way to welcome the seasons. Parties may center on a porch, field, outdoor fireplace, or cooking pit.

- *Picnics.* Pack the following items for a perfect picnic: salt and pepper, napkins, corkscrew, sharp knife, serving spoons, small plates, cups or glasses and cutlery for each person, a variety of finger foods and sandwiches, fresh strawberries, grapes and cheese, water, wine, or other beverages, blanket or tablecloth, and a bag for the trash. Picnickers with young children may wish to include a small first-aid kit.

The Guest List

After you have chosen the event, theme, and date, your next task should be the guest list. There is an art to creating a pleasant guest list, and the smaller your event, the more careful you must be in selecting the guests. For a general dinner conversation, it is wise to limit the number of guests to eight. Select guests who will mix well, or have something in common. I have found it pleasant to try to add one new person to a group. Avoid inviting guests who dominate the conversation (unless they are quite interesting or amusing). Also avoid those who chatter endlessly, or who sit moodily. Unfortunately I have found that most often these types of people are related to me in some way, and I therefore have no choice in the matter, but whenever possible, it is always best to refrain from inflicting unnecessary pain on one's dinner guests.

Planning the Menu

After the event, theme, date, and guests have been chosen, I have found it most helpful to use a guide as I plan any party with more than six guests. I am less likely to leave out a small detail, which, I have learned, is often the difference between an evening to be endured and an evening to be remembered.

Great care must be taken when selecting the menu. The flavors and aromas must complement each other, and there should be a good balance of colors, textures, and flavors. Avoid choosing menu items that are similar, such as rice and potatoes. Consider portions carefully. Balance a heavy meal with a light dessert and

Menu

vice versa. Remember: *The presentation of the meal is nearly as important as the quality of the food.* For beginning hostesses, simple tried-and-true recipes work best. And, most importantly, *never* experiment with new recipes at a dinner party, for your guests may thus become unsuspecting victims!

Use the following list to plan your menu.

Cocktails:

_____

Appetizers:

_____

Main dish (meat):

_____

Potato or rice accompaniment:

_____

Vegetables:

_____

Salads:

_____

Relishes or sauces:

_____

Bread:

_____

Dessert:

_____

Beverages (before, during, and after dinner):

_____

Garnishes:

_____

Wines or after-dinner cordials:

_____

Coffee:

_____

Table Appointments

Having planned the menu, I determine the amount of food needed according to the size and appetites of my guest list. I then begin to consider my table appointments and other necessary items using the list on the following pages as a reminder. The first sight of the table plays an important role for any meal. It sets the mood for the evening, and therefore it is essential that the setting be just right for the occasion. Whether crisp and sophisticated, softly flowing with lace and flowers, or warm and homey, the table should complement the decor of the room and form a focal point. There is nothing quite like a clean white linen tablecloth, crisply starched, with heavy, white damask, folded napkins on a dinner party table. And all things should *sparkle*. The silver and glassware should shine like the full moon over the mighty Mississippi. An elegant array of either candles or flowers adds the finishing touch to the table setting, creating an atmosphere that cannot be equaled by any form. A mirror in the dining room always adds ambience to the sparkle.

Consider outdoor and entrance decorations, too, as this serves to set the mood and atmosphere as guests approach the house.

Pay special attention to the powder room, making sure it is clean and fresh smelling. Put out soaps and pretty hand towels for guests to use. A small vase of fresh flowers or lit candles can add charm and fragrance to the powder room.

Three things to avoid . . . too little or too much light (soft, but not *too* low is best), high centerpieces (guests cannot see each other), and a too-serious hostess (it's a party, not a wake!). Relax. Be kind, friendly, and easy.

Once the dining is over, be prepared to catch the "low" moment of the party. It is often that time just after the meal, before the party retires to the parlor for coffee and after-dinner drinks. The clever hostess rings in music, games, or some other form of amusement before a party has time to curl up and die.

Using the following guide, I prepare my table appointments, and since *nothing* is left until the last moment, I am carefree, calm, and prepared to enjoy a delightful evening with my guests. *It is simply not worth the trouble of throwing a lavish party if you, the hostess, cannot enjoy yourself!*

China:

_____

Glassware:

_____

Silver flatware:

_____

Silver serving pieces:

_____

Salt and pepper containers:

_____

Table linens and napkins:

_____

Centerpieces:

_____

Candles:

_____

Leaves and flowers for decorating:

_____

Serving spoons:

_____

Place cards:

_____

Wine or champagne glasses:

_____

Ashtrays and matches:

_____

Powder room necessities:

_____

Provisions for coats, hats, and wraps:

_____

As I complete this list, it gives me the opportunity to inspect and polish any tarnished silver, clean soiled linens, and prepare my china and crystal for perfect display. These things should be tended to immediately, as you will be distracted with other important details as the party date approaches.

Finally, I make a schedule of the chores to be done before my guests arrive:

Cleaning chores to be done:

_____

_____

_____

_____

Details that can be tended to—

The week before:

_____

_____

_____

Two days before:

_____

_____

_____

The day before:

_____

_____

_____

The morning of:

_____

_____

_____

Last minute:

_____

_____

_____

Ideally, the last-minute chore should be tending only to yourself to ensure that your appearance is pleasing; that you are calm, assured, poised, and prepared to be the most gracious hostess possible. I am reminded of the words of Dear Aunt Middle Mary before one of her lavish soirees: "The hostess must give the appearance of a duck sailing on lake, calm and serene on the surface, but paddling like the dickens underneath."

Table Setting and Seating

The host is always at the head of the table, while the hostess is seated at the other end. The guest of honor sits at the right of the host and is always served first at every course.

The table linen and napkins must be spotless white and neatly pressed. The table setting should be geometric, with the centerpiece in the exact center; candlesticks and settings balanced, parallel, and at equal distance; and place settings in identical order. Candles may be used at dinner, but never at lunch. Use at least two candelabra or four candles. Remember that dining room lighting should flatter your guests more than your furnishings.

"It's not so important that you marry a man who can distinguish a cocktail fork from a salad fork, but rather, seek a man who can afford to buy you both. You can teach him which is which."

—AUNT MIDDLE MARY

Plates, glasses, silver, and individual pieces should be in the identical relationship for each setting. Place silver 2 inches from the edge of the table in parallel lines. A plate should have designs straight for the person in front of it. Forks (except small cocktail forks) are placed to the left of the plate. Knives, spoons, cocktail fork, et cetera, go to the right of the plate, in reverse order of use. Those to be used first are placed farthest from the plate. The water glass is placed at the tip of the dinner knife. The bread-and-butter plate is placed to the upper left of the plate, with the butter knife either horizontally or vertically across it. Napkins are placed to the left of the fork, not under it. For formal dinners, the napkin is sometimes placed on a place plate.

When serving, all food should be passed, placed, and removed from the left. All beverages are placed, poured, and removed at the right. Dishes containing food should be held low enough so as to enable guests to help themselves. The handle of the serving fork or spoon should be toward the guest, with the fork to the left of the person.

The server should remove the dinner plate with the right hand and the bread-and-butter plate or salad plate with the left hand.

Setting the table

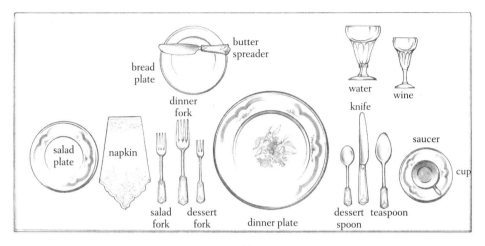

Proper table setting

Water glasses should be filled without removing them from the table. A napkin should be held in the left hand slightly under the lip of the pitcher.

The guest of honor, or the hostess, should be served first. Then those to the right of the first person should be served, continuing around the table. Dishes should be served (or passed) in this order: main dish, vegetable or accompaniment, sauces, bread, relishes, and salads. Use a white napkin, folded in a square, in placing and removing dishes. Remove dishes in the following order: main dish, accompanying dishes, dinner plates, bread-and-butter plates, salad plates together, relishes, and salt and peppers. Never stack dishes on one another. Crumb the table with a folded napkin and a small plate after the main course.

The Buffet Table

An attractive centerpiece should be placed in the center of the table, and each dish should have the appropriate serving utensils.

When planning the arrangement of a buffet table, the following order is traditionally used:

Plates

Side dishes

Main dish

Vegetables

Salad

Bread

Butter

Relishes

Forks

Knives

Napkins

Place drinks on a separate table to avoid spills and crowding. Make sure there is plenty of seating. Position chairs in groups of three or more so that your guests may enjoy each other's company while dining.

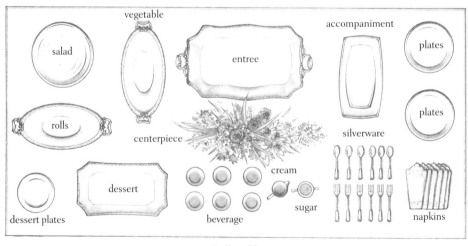

Buffet table

A Little Common Sense

Never place a clock in the dining room—time is no issue when you entertain.

The Dinner Conversation

As the hostess, it is your duty to steer the conversation away from extremely controversial subjects or subjects which might embarrass anyone. Break up the "lecture" when it begins to bore, or a heated discussion when it becomes uncomfortable for others present. Never let anyone at your dinner table commit the crimes of etiquette for which the best solution is for the perpetrator to disappear from the face of the earth. I remember Dear Mother interrupting the most inappropriate, insulting remarks of one dinner guest at her table by accidentally (on purpose) knocking her own red wine glass onto her very beautiful Irish lace tablecloth. A race to rescue the linen was on by those guests seated near her, and as she calmly tended to the matter, she prompted my father to tell his latest adventure story. In mere moments the situation was defused and all was forgotten. Afterward, my sisters and I questioned her judgment on ruining her own expensive tablecloth; her reply was simply, "Things can be replaced, people and their feelings cannot."

In your role as hostess, it is also your responsibility to keep the topics of conversation shifting. When conversation lags, bring up a subject of general interest to all. Reading magazines and, of course, newspapers a day or two before your party will give you interesting ideas as topics of conversations. Avoid discussions of personal ills, the exploits of your children, or any new purchases. Likewise, do not attempt to eulogize your dishes, or apologize that they did not turn out to your liking. This is in extreme bad taste, as is the vaunting of the excellence of your wines. A safe subject is always what is happening to the other person.

Serving Wine

The host pours, and should pour a very small amount of wine into his own glass to remove any sediment. He then fills each glass three-quarters full. The bottle is next placed on the table, wrapped in a white napkin. Appetizer or dessert wines should be served in a cocktail glass, white wine should be served in a medium-size wine-glass, and red wine is best served in a goblet. Sparkling wines should be served in a medium-size stemmed glass. Toasting glasses should be as thin as possible, but also large. These should only be filled partially, in order to let the bouquet escape freely. If it is an old wine, it is best to decant it beforehand to separate the deposit which results from age and to allow the aromas to develop freely.

Aperitifs (vermouth, Dubonnet, sherry) may be served before the meal. White wines (Sauternes, Rhine) are served with fish, shellfish, or poultry. Meat, pâté de foie gras, cheese, and nuts bring out the finer qualities of red wine. Avoid serving vinegar-dressed salads or sweet vegetables with wine. The flavors are abrasive.

Sweet wines (port, Madeira) or cordials are served with desserts or after the meal. If several wines are to be served, begin with the "younger" or newer vintages, leading up to the heavier, older, and noble bottles.

White wines, sparkling wines, pink wines, and very dry sherry or Madeira should be served chilled. Red wines, medium and rich sherry, Madeira, port, Marsala, and spirits are served at room temperature.

Toasting

A proper toast helps us to live in and appreciate the moment. Our hearts and souls are connected as we collectively share appreciation for family and friends and all of life's blessings.

The host always offers the first toast. To gain the attention of those present it is customary for him to lightly tap on the edge of a glass. The host then stands and makes a concise and fitting spoken toast and raises his glass to the honoree, or simply in the air if the toast is not for a person. Other guests merely raise their glasses in recognition. Then guests take a sip of wine. The recipient of the toast *sits and does not drink himself.* He may respond with a toast of his own.

In a large celebration where there is a dais (such as a wedding meal), only those people on the dais may propose toasts.

"Eat thy bread with joy, and drink thy wine with a merry heart."
—Ecclesiastes 9:10

Favorite Toasts from the Judge

☞ May the roof above us never fall in. And may the friends gathered below it never fall out.

☞ May all single men be married, and all married men be happy.

☞ To Woman: The fairest work of the Great Author; the edition is wonderful and no man should be without a copy.

☞ May the most you wish for, be the least you get.

☞ May the saddest day of your future be no worse than the happiest day of your past.

How to Make a Speech

Be sincere. Be brief. Be seated.

Table Manners by Ten

All residents of Dunwoody House mastered these manners by the age of ten.

1. Don't sit until the host does, unless you have been instructed to do so.

2. Sit straight up in your chair, never leaning back or forward. Never let your elbows touch the table. When eating, do not bring your face toward the plate, but rather, bring the utensil up to your mouth.

3. Never do anything until the host does it first. This includes sitting, putting your napkin in your lap, picking up your fork, putting your napkin on the table, and leaving.

4. When bread is passed, take only one slice. Using the butter knife on the butter dish, take some butter and put it on your bread plate. Tear a bite-size piece off your bread and butter it. Eat with delight. Continue in this manner. Never butter the entire slice of bread at once. Never cut your bread with a knife. It should always be broken by hand.

5. Use your utensils from the outside in. To begin the appetizer, use the fork farthest to the outside. When the next course arrives, use the next outermost fork (or utensil), and so on.

6. Here is the proper technique for right-handers to use the fork and knife (left-handers may reverse these directions): Hold the fork in the left hand and the knife in the right. With the tines facing downward (curving toward you), hold down an end piece of meat. Gently, using a sawing motion, cut the meat near the tines of the fork, so that you have one bite-size piece. Then, lay the knife down on the right edge of the plate, without allowing it to touch the table, and switch the fork (which holds the bite-size piece of meat) to your right hand. Bring it up to your mouth, chew quietly, and swallow when the meat is sufficiently masticated. Once a utensil has been used, never allow it to touch the table again. Leave it on the plate.

7. When eating soup, spoon away from you. Lower your spoon gently into the soup, taking care not to bang the bottom of the bowl. (Imagine a room full of people banging their bowl bottoms!) Fill the spoon about three-quarters full of soup, bring it to your mouth, and sip it from the side of the spoon, being

A Little Common Sense

If you suffer some horrible embarrassment which you may laugh about later . . . go ahead and laugh about it now.

For truly, he who can laugh at himself will never cease to be amused.

careful not to make any sounds. When your soup runs low, it is acceptable to tip the bowl away from you to capture the last bit, but don't do this more than twice.

"Don't eat in front of friends unless you have enough to share."

8. Refrain from making *any* noise while eating, chew with your mouth closed, and don't talk with food in your mouth. Always use your napkin before and after drinking.

9. When finished, place your knife and fork on the plate so that they are parallel to each other, at the eleven o'clock position (a diagonal from bottom right to top left, with the points facing away from you). Place your napkin on the table next to your plate when everyone else is finished.

10. If you must leave the table, excuse yourself first.

11. When in doubt what to do, follow the hostess. Try to pace the eating of your meal with your hostess. Follow her for cues.

12. And lastly, remember to be poised and polite at all times.

Learn to "Dine"—Not to "Eat"

Nothing is such a test of good breeding as behavior at the table. Indeed, I have been known to put many a child in front of a mirror in the hope of teaching him the difference between "dining" and "eating." Master the art of bringing food to your mouth, instead of your mouth to the food, and practice masticating until you do it with your lips closed and without disturbing gurgling or smacking noises. Eat slowly without gulping, and try to make your conversation interesting. We should be able to feed ourselves inoffensively and in a manner entirely secondary to conversation. Our dinner companion should be impressed with our engrossing conversation, interesting eyes, and pleasant, melodious voice, and entirely oblivious to the fact that we are eating. An inconspicuous eater has easy, quiet table manners, and uses two hands only when one won't suffice.

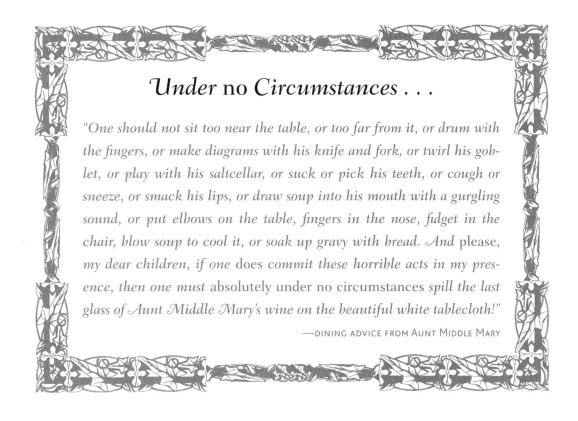

Under no Circumstances . . .

"One should not sit too near the table, or too far from it, or drum with the fingers, or make diagrams with his knife and fork, or twirl his goblet, or play with his saltcellar, or suck or pick his teeth, or cough or sneeze, or smack his lips, or draw soup into his mouth with a gurgling sound, or put elbows on the table, fingers in the nose, fidget in the chair, blow soup to cool it, or soak up gravy with bread. And please, my dear children, if one does commit these horrible acts in my presence, then one must absolutely under no circumstances spill the last glass of Aunt Middle Mary's wine on the beautiful white tablecloth!"

—DINING ADVICE FROM AUNT MIDDLE MARY

Holiday Entertaining

Precious children—a final note—remember as we celebrate the meaningful times of the year with a special dinner at home, we must always include those friends who may not be near family members or unable to travel. Certainly one of the kindest things we can do is to invite our "orphaned" friends to our home to share in the joy of the holiday. For by so doing, it always adds to the pleasure of our own day. In the words of Epictetus, "At feasts, remember that you are entertaining two guests: *body and soul.* What you give to the body, you presently lose; what you give to the soul, you keep forever."

The Proper Tea Party

"In serving tea, the table should be arranged before any visitors arrive. Its cover may be a linen tea cloth embroidered or trimmed with lace, while the cups and saucers, with the spoon resting in each saucer, the thin slices of lemon, the small wafers, cakes or sandwiches on plates or pretty doilies, should be artistically arranged upon it. The tea kettle should be in its place, the teapot just in front of it. The cream pitcher and sugar bowl should be within convenient reach. If the hostess pours the tea, she allows the guest to put in the sugar and cream for themselves. If she expects many visitors, then there will be wisdom in asking a friend to pour tea for her."

—*Ladies' Home Journal, 1897*

The Guest Book

The keeping of a "guest book" is one of those peculiar rituals that you will have no sense of appreciation for, until it is too late. So, dear children, I am writing this down to tell you how lovely a thing it can be. I have just spent the most delightful evening reviewing my collection of guest books, and short of the presence of the guests themselves, I cannot imagine a more sublime evening. From my first guest book, which Dear Mother saved from my debutante ball although I was only seventeen at the time, the names in the roster bring tears to my eyes, as nearly all of those contained therein have passed on now. But the handwritten words from family and such dear friends make my heart leap, and I find myself holding my own breath as I read down the roll of guests. It's as if that night is frozen in time, and like a photograph, I can recall the details so vividly. In those precious days of abundance, before this horrid war pillaged the South, times were so very sophisticated, elegant, and lovely. And though I fear at times that those carefree days of splendor shall never return, they indeed do, every time I pick up one of my guest books. We need to live a *considered* life. A guest book is one of the surest ways I know of to accomplish this.

"Always stand at the doorway and wave good-bye until your departing guests are out of sight."

—Aunt Middle Mary

Famous guest books include the Vanderbilts', known for the clever rhymes guests compose, which need no explanation to its stunning self-importance, and the Teeter family of Norfolk, Connecticut (more to my liking), which has demonstrated a perennially frivolous bent with a book in which guests are expected to sign their names and then, with their eyes firmly shut, draw a pig. Also amusing is Sarah Hornaday, Dear Mother's school-days friend and a sedulous keeper of guest books, who is known for occasionally

Party Notes

Event	Date	Theme

forgetting to ask departing guests to sign her cherished book and has been reportedly seen dashing down the driveway after them, hallooing and waving the book aloft.

A guest book bespeaks happy times, whether at a formal ball or a simple summertime supper. The guest book should be granted a place of prominence in the household: usually on a table by the front door, or in the doorway of the front parlor. In a well-tended guest book one reads a family's history from decade to decade, as visitors too young to write for themselves have their hands drawn in outline by their doting parents, and as time passes by, even *their children's hands* find their way into the cherished book. Some of my fondest memories have been of entertaining family, friends, old and new, and even strangers in my home. In the annals of my guest books I have record of them all. And those precious hand scrawls of all shapes, sizes, and varieties, like the people who inscribed them, are as unique and unforgettable as memories can be.

And so, my precious children, you must begin your guest books right away! Your next-door neighbors and your mother would do well as the first inscribers.

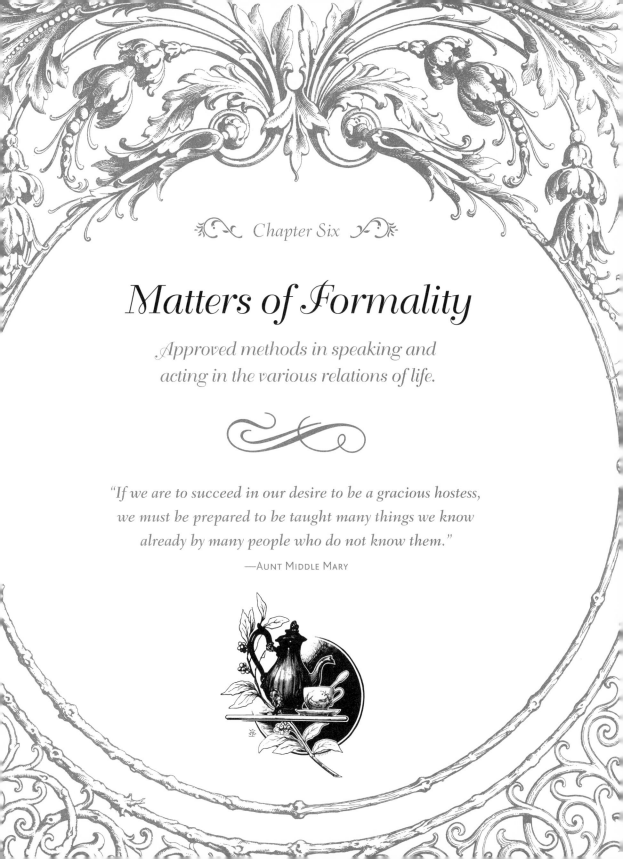

Chapter Six

Matters of Formality

*Approved methods in speaking and
acting in the various relations of life.*

*"If we are to succeed in our desire to be a gracious hostess,
we must be prepared to be taught many things we know
already by many people who do not know them."*

—AUNT MIDDLE MARY

A Hostess's Guide to Fundamental Hospitality

The perfection of hospitable entertainment is to offer the best to visitors; show a polite regard to their wishes; and give precedence in all matters of comfort and convenience. A proper hostess must never reveal her frustrations or dislike regarding visitors and their needs. She must resist all urges to seem anything other than delighted to receive guests into her home. Social tact is perhaps best defined as making your company feel *at home,* even though you wish *they were.* A woman of true distinction knows that manners must be guided by the knowledge that anything which is upsetting or irritating to one's guests is not in good form. But, of course, as Dear Mother taught us all, good breeding consists of concealing how much we think of ourselves and how little we think of others.

On the other hand, to press people to eat more than they wish, insist on ceaseless activities for guests, and to try to force people on one another can only be described as *vulgar hospitality.* Harassing guests in this manner creates an uncomfortable sense of indebtedness. Too much hospitality makes everyone sick of everyone else. Many know how to please, but know not when they have ceased to give pleasure.

Excess of ceremony shows want of good breeding. That civility is best which excludes all superfluous ceremony. There is no social duty which the Supreme Lawgiver more strenuously urges, than hospitality and kindness to strangers.

The Rules of Good Conduct
Which Govern Good Society

Manners are often viewed, by those who lack them, as a particular set of silly rules that arrogant people refer to, in order to make those whom they view as beneath them feel out of their class. On the contrary, the first rule of good manners is to never insult anyone intentionally. Simply defined, manners—etiquette—is the way civilized human beings behave around one another to minimize conflict. It is the custom of polite society.

Proper etiquette is not a set of rigid formal rules, but rather an informal agreement among people, a distillation of human conduct which has developed over the course of time. As man has progressed in civility, the need for etiquette, or simple decency became increasingly clear. Because rules, if well written and consistently observed, do not repress; rather, they liberate. They are not a sign of weakness, but a symbol of a faith, and they allow us all to appreciate and enjoy one another for our positive aspects.

In good breeding, the *manner* always adorns and dignifies the *matter*. The manner is often as important as the matter, sometimes more so; a favor may make an enemy, and an injury may make a friend, according to the different manner in which they are done. Gentleness of manner with firmness of mind is, perhaps, a short but full description of human perfection.

The Etiquette of Introductions

Correct introductions are a matter of remembering names and of proper presentation of the age, sex, and prestige of your acquain-

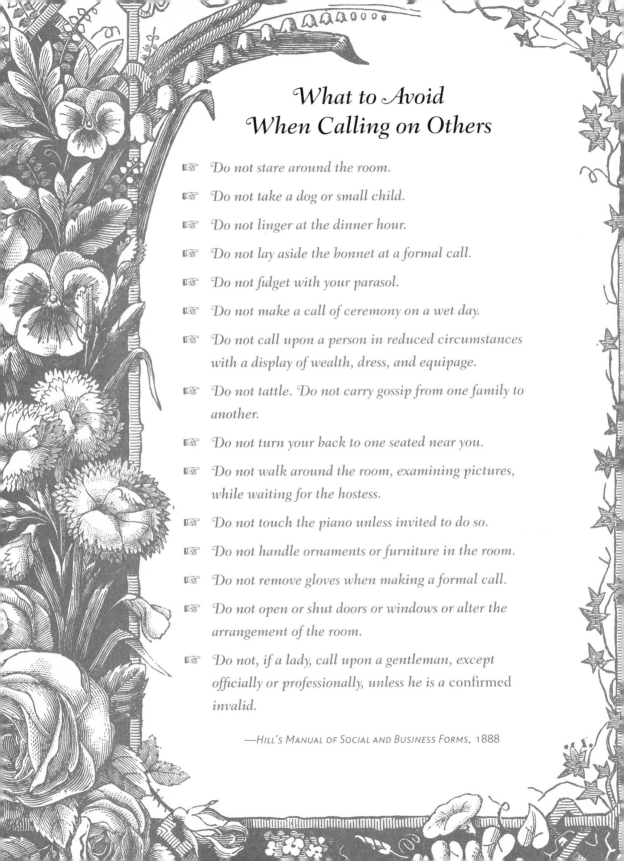

What to Avoid
When Calling on Others

☞ Do not stare around the room.

☞ Do not take a dog or small child.

☞ Do not linger at the dinner hour.

☞ Do not lay aside the bonnet at a formal call.

☞ Do not fidget with your parasol.

☞ Do not make a call of ceremony on a wet day.

☞ Do not call upon a person in reduced circumstances with a display of wealth, dress, and equipage.

☞ Do not tattle. Do not carry gossip from one family to another.

☞ Do not turn your back to one seated near you.

☞ Do not walk around the room, examining pictures, while waiting for the hostess.

☞ Do not touch the piano unless invited to do so.

☞ Do not handle ornaments or furniture in the room.

☞ Do not remove gloves when making a formal call.

☞ Do not open or shut doors or windows or alter the arrangement of the room.

☞ Do not, if a lady, call upon a gentleman, except officially or professionally, unless he is a confirmed invalid.

—*HILL'S MANUAL OF SOCIAL AND BUSINESS FORMS*, 1888

tances. In all introductions, the gentleman is presented to the lady: "Miss Spalding, may I present Mr. Willingham." A hostess or mutual acquaintance may do the presenting. A younger person is always presented to an older person. "Dear Mother, I would like you to meet my school friend Miss Marianne Gilliam. Marianne, this is my Dear Mother, Mrs. Wylly."

Introduce the unknown to the famed. "Mr. Vanderbilt, may I present Miss Harriet Anderson." On highly formal occasions, guests are announced to the room by the butler as they enter: "Mr. and Mrs. Wesley John Griffin." (This, of course, has the added benefit of helping buffoons, such as myself, recall the names of previous acquaintances.)

Where many people are in a room, never lead anyone around like a dog on a leash introducing her to everyone in the room. Choose one small group where you think she will be on comfortable footing with something in common. Introduce her by calling her name once and following with a conversation starter such as: "Penelope, this is Thadius Vanderhooten who doesn't believe in income tax."

Rules of Precedence

It is well to remember the "Ladies First" slogan. There are some exceptions, but not many. Except in the case of darkness or actual danger of tripping, the woman precedes the man ascending or descending stairs.

The woman precedes her escort into a restaurant and to the table, but follows the maître d'. She leads the way when leaving the restaurant. She enters all conveyances first, but the man precedes her when leaving them so that he may assist her when alighting.

When Attending the Theater

EDITOR'S NOTE: *Mrs. Dunwoody attended the opera whenever possible. Her rules of theater etiquette are observed to this day.*

When attending the theater it is well to remember that the person with the tickets precedes. The hostess precedes down the aisle in the case of a feminine party. With two women, the guest follows the usher. The man, in the case of a man and woman attending the theater, precedes the lady if there is no usher, but she may go ahead if an usher is showing them to their seats. A woman never takes an aisle seat when with a man. When two men and two women attend the theater, one of the women may take her place followed by one of the men, and then the other woman, as it is not necessary for both men to stand aside to let the women enter first. The most important thing about theater manners is not to annoy or inconvenience others in the theater. One is also advised not to be late, rustle one's program, or eat garlic before the performance.

At the Dinner Party

At formal dinners, the hostess enters the dining room with the principal guest of the party. The host accompanies the wife of this guest, and enters the dining room first, followed by the other dinner partners. The hostess enters last with the guest of honor. After a formal dinner, the hostess rises first, attracting the attention of the wife of the honor guest. Then she leads the way from the dining room to the drawing room, or wherever the coffee is to be served. Informal dinners do not require observance of special rules.

Street Etiquette

When a gentleman walks the street, it is proper to offer a lady his arm, particularly in the evening, and it should always be the right arm. People passing should observe the law of "turn to the right," and in this way the lady would not be jostled. It is always proper for a gentleman walking alone to give the lady, or gentleman with a lady, the inside of the walk.

A lady walks quietly through the streets, seeing and hearing nothing that she ought not to, recognizing acquaintances with a courteous bow, and friends with words of greeting. She is always unobtrusive, never talking loudly, or laughing boisterously, or doing anything to attract the attention of the passersby. She walks along in her own quiet, ladylike way, and by her preoccupation, is secure from any annoyance. A true lady in the street, as in the parlor, is modest, discreet, kind, and obliging.

"Yankees don't know any better, so always be kind to them."

—Aunt Middle Mary

Becoming a Belle

It is well known by all, that Southern belles take pride in their hospitality, manners, charm, and the art of being a woman in the South. Young women growing up in the South are most fortunate; for there is never a lack of ideal ladylike behavior to observe, learn from, and emulate.

One simply cannot consider oneself a Southern belle, unless the following behavior is strictly observed:

☞ A lady is never rude to anyone.

☞ A lady will not dress in an odd way as to attract attention or remarks.

☞ A lady in public walks wrapped in a mantle of proper reserve, so impenetrable that insult and coarse familiarity shrink from her.

- ☞ A lady carries herself with dignity, but never in such a way to make others think she feels superior to them.

- ☞ A lady is kind to all people, and carries with her a congenial atmosphere which puts all at ease.

- ☞ A lady refrains from discussing anything unpleasant or indecent.

- ☞ A lady does not smoke, or bite her fingernails.

- ☞ A lady is always concerned with the health and happiness of those around her and will do everything she can to see that they are properly attended to.

- ☞ A lady is never late (lest it give her suitors time to count up her faults).

- ☞ A lady's integrity is never at question.

- ☞ A lady understands that inflexibility is the hallmark of the tiny mind.

- ☞ A lady possesses a sense of humor and can easily laugh at herself, but never at others.

The Code of a Gentleman

Too many of us assume that a rich man is a gentleman. No qualification could be farther from the truth, since the quality of a gentleman is measured by what he *is* and never by what he *has*. Fundamentally, it is a man's code of honor, no matter how "polished" he may seem, that determines a gentleman.

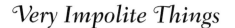

Very Impolite Things

- ☞ Staring at anyone—man, woman, or child—in a marked manner.
- ☞ Pointing at others.
- ☞ Leaving a stranger without a seat.
- ☞ Correcting parents, or persons older than yourself.
- ☞ Want of respect and reverence for seniors.
- ☞ Having a laugh at someone else's expense.
- ☞ Laughing at the mistakes or accidents of others.
- ☞ Not helping someone who is in obvious need of assistance.
- ☞ Rude remarks.
- ☞ Swearing or talking uproariously.
- ☞ Spitting on the street.
- ☞ Talking when others are reading.
- ☞ Reading when others are talking.
- ☞ Reading aloud in company without being asked.
- ☞ Receiving a present without an expression of gratitude.
- ☞ Whispering or laughing in the house of God.
- ☞ Losing your temper in public. (I find my garden is a much more appropriate place for such outbursts and eruptions.)
- ☞ Cutting your fingernails in company.
- ☞ Being late: It implies that your time is more important than others'.
- ☞ Forgetting your mother's birthday (December 22).

A Gentleman . . .

☞ Never takes advantage of the poor, helpless, or ignorant and assumes that no gentleman will take advantage of him.

☞ When in company, never puts his hands to any part of the body not usually discovered.

☞ Is always considerate of the feelings of others no matter what the station of others may be.

☞ Never fails to offer the easiest and best seat in the room to an invalid, elderly person, or a lady.

☞ Does not "sponge" off of others, but pays for, or earns his own way.

☞ Does not name drop and avoids the mention of what things cost.

☞ Does not talk of, or make a display of his wealth.

☞ Does not allude to conquests which he may (or may not) have made with the ladies.

☞ Dislikes the mention of money, and out of business hours, never speaks of it.

☞ Never discusses his family affairs, or his wife or her appearance, either in public or with acquaintances.

☞ Never treats his wife with disrespect in the company of others (including children and servants).

☞ No matter who he may be, or how high or low his position in life may be, never besmirches his wife's name, for in so doing he besmirches still more his own, and proves that he *is not, was not,* and *never will be,* a gentleman.

"He whose manners are put on only in company is a veneered gentleman, not a real one."

☞ Does not go to a lady's house if he is affected by alcohol.

☞ Spits not into the fire, in the presence of others.

☞ Kills no vermin, as fleas, lice, ticks, and such in the sight of others; and when any filth or thick spittle is seen, he puts his foot dexterously upon it.

☞ Runs not in the streets; neither goes too slowly; kicks not the earth with his feet; and does not go upon the toes in a dancing fashion.

☞ Does not walk around with his mouth hanging open, lest he be thought a fool.

☞ Does not lose control of his temper, in fact, his own self-control under difficult circumstances is his main ascendancy over others who impulsively betray every emotion which animates them.

—*GEORGE WASHINGTON'S RULES OF CIVILITY & DECENT BEHAVIOR* (SELECTED)

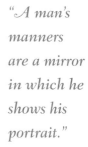

"A man's manners are a mirror in which he shows his portrait."
—GOETHE
(1749–1834)

The born gentleman's manners are an integral part of him and they are the same whether he is in the ballroom or the bedroom, whether he is speaking to the queen of England or the laundry maid. To be born a gentleman is an accident. To die one is an achievement.

It is my hope that these instructions may be of some use to you and how you present your person. Judge Dunwoody would often tease me, saying, "Yes, dear, it is most helpful to know the proper way to behave, so one can decide whether or not to be proper."

The Art of Conversation

Ideal conversation must be a civil give-and-take exchange of thoughts, ideas, and interesting information. If you dread meeting strangers because you fear you have nothing to say, you would do well to remember that most of the crimes of conversation are committed not by those who talk too little, but by those who talk too much. Avoid being thought of as the silly girl who never has an unexpressed thought in her head. Better to close your mouth and remain a mystery, than to open your mouth and erase all doubt. As George Eliot wrote, "Blessed is the man who, having nothing to say, abstains from giving in words evidence of the fact."

Think before you speak. Of all things, banish egotism from your conversation and never think of entertaining people with your

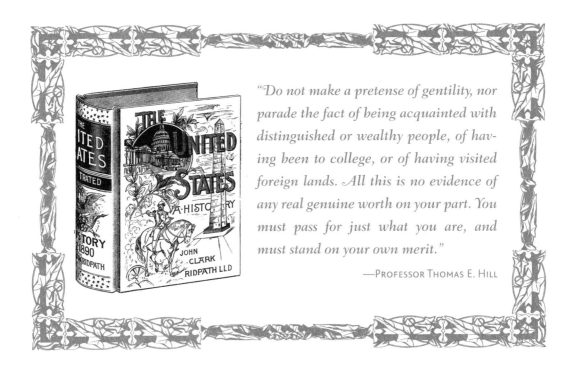

"Do not make a pretense of gentility, nor parade the fact of being acquainted with distinguished or wealthy people, of having been to college, or of having visited foreign lands. All this is no evidence of any real genuine worth on your part. You must pass for just what you are, and must stand on your own merit."

—Professor Thomas E. Hill

own personal concerns or private affairs; like the recounting of a dream, though they are interesting to you, they are tedious and impertinent to everybody else. Never tell a story in which you are the hero. It is far more impressive when others discover your good qualities without your help. Wise men may not always be silent, but *they do know when* to be.

Never interrupt the speaker; it is considered very rude. Whoever interrupts the conversation of others to make a display of his fund of knowledge, makes notorious his own stock of ignorance. Recollect that the object of conversation is to entertain and amuse.

"Better to close your mouth and remain a mystery, than to open your mouth and erase all doubt."
—JUDGE DUNWOODY

Remember that saying something once is effective; twice is boring. Refrain from commencing a conversation by an allusion to the weather. Do not use profanity, vulgar terms, or language that will bring the blush to any person. Take care that your tone of voice is neither loud or unpleasant and refrain from appearing too common, as do those fools who resist all inclinations to enunciate properly.

Always look people in the face when you speak to them; not doing so is thought to imply conscious guilt; besides that, you lose the advantage of observing by their countenances what impressions your discourse makes upon them. In conversation, a person's manner should always be carefully observed, for it is by the observation of this subtle communication that we are better able to communicate with one another. If your listener begins to look away from your eyes or face while you are speaking, seems distracted, or checks his watch or surroundings, this is your cue to politely end the conversation and carry on with your respective affairs. *No behavior on our part is more self-centered than the demand to speak and the refusal to listen.* Such behavior is a root cause of most interpersonal conflict.

Tell stories very seldom and never but when they are apt and very short. That is about all that one person should inflict on company. People seem not to understand that their opinion of the world is also a confession of character. Frequent recourse to narrative betrays great want of imagination.

Neither repeat or receive scandal willingly; as in robbery, the receiver is always thought as bad as the thief. And of course, we must resist all urges to spit out gossip, as compelling as it might be, for, like a boomerang, it has a nasty habit of smacking one back in the face. Remember—no one gets hurt from words we don't say.

Let your manner, your air, your terms, and your tone of voice be soft and gentle, easy and natural. Good nature is more agreeable in conversation, even more than wit, and gives a certain air to the countenance which is more amiable than beauty.

Use palliatives when you contradict, such as, "I may be mistaken," "I am not sure, but I believe," "I should think," et cetera. Finish any argument with some little good-humored pleasantry, to show that you are neither hurt yourself, nor meant to hurt your antagonist. The secret to diffusing all uncomfortable situations is humor. Wit makes its own welcome and levels all distinctions.

Elders justly expect from young people a degree of deference and regard. You should be full and easy with them as with people of your own years; but your manner must be different; more respect must be implied; and it is not amiss to insinuate, that from them you expect to learn. Do not run your own present humor and disposition indiscriminately against everybody; but observe, conform to, and adopt theirs. As Plato said, "The more pleasures of the body fade away, the greater to me is the pleasure and charm of conversation."

Words can be slippery and lethal. Choose them carefully. The Bible tells us that man's sharpest weapon is his tongue. We spend

A Little Common Sense

Reputation is a large bubble that bursts
when you try to blow it up yourself.

three years learning how to use it and the rest of our lives learning how to control it. Remember, a closed mouth gathers no feet.

Over the years I have observed that the secret to excellent conversation lies not in what you say, but rather in what you do. *Be a good listener.* To do all the talking and not be willing to listen is a form of greed. Do not just listen to what others say, consider *why* they are saying it and respond accordingly. Others are not nearly as interested in what we have to say as they are in what they want to say to us. People like to talk about themselves, and so if you leave the meeting, and your companion has just spent the last quarter hour telling you about himself, and he leaves knowing nothing of you, chances are he will think well of you, like you, become excited at seeing you again, because he will walk away feeling very good about himself, perhaps never even realizing that the reason was the rapt attention paid to him and the telling of his story. People will forget what you say and do, but they will never forget *how you make them feel.*

Everyone, even a simpleton, has at least one interesting fact to know, or humorous pleasantry to discover. *Search for the hidden gem in all persons.* Ask yourself, "What does this person know which I don't know?" Make a game of it. "What can I learn from him?" To your surprise, you will often find that if you pay close attention to what others are saying, you will find yourself *genuinely* interested and involved in their conversation. Occasionally you may wish to make a comment or ask a pertinent question, but never give any information about yourself. *When we listen, we learn. Just listen.* That's why the good Lord gave you two ears and only one mouth: to listen twice as much as you speak. The tongue weighs practically nothing, and yet so few people can hold it.

Unconsciousness of self is not so much unselfishness as it is the mental ability to extinguish all thought of oneself—exactly as one turns out the light. Simplicity is like it, in that it also has a quality of self-effacement, but it really means a love of the essential and of directness. Simple people put no trimmings on their phrases *or* on their manners. But remember: Simplicity is not crudeness, or anything like it. On the contrary, simplicity of speech and manners means language in its purest, most limpid form, and manners of such perfection that they do not suggest "manners" at all. As Samuel Johnson wrote, "That is the happiest conversation where there is no competition, no vanity, but a calm, quiet interchange of sentiments."

The Art of Letter Writing

The German poet Goethe once said that letters are among the most significant memorials a person could leave behind. Indeed, letters are above all useful as a means of expressing the ideal self; and no other method of communication is quite so good for this purpose. For it is within our letters that we can reform without practice, beg without humiliation, and snip and shape our experiences to the measure of our own desires.

Recently, my dear friend Mr. Henry Miller wrote, "It does me good to write a letter which is not a response to a demand, but rather a gratuitous letter, so to speak, which has accumulated in me like the waters of a reservoir." What a charming sentiment! Well and truly I can tell you that I have been on both the giving and receiving ends of the art of letter writing, and can't imagine a more delightful way to express the emotion that wells up within my soul. Perhaps no other activity can move the soul of a loved one more than that of a thoughtfully written letter. It is the least expensive gift we can give, and yet to the recipient, its worth is often priceless.

The Letter Everyone Loves to Receive

The letter we all love to receive is one that carries so much of the writer's personality that she seems to be sitting beside us, looking at us directly, and talking just as she really would, could she have magically appeared before us.

Each letter I receive from cousin Corabelle is one of those perfect letters which seem almost to have written themselves, so easily do the words flow. Her letters tell not only what she has been doing, but also what she has been thinking and feeling. There is often a lot about me in the letter as well, nice things that make me feel rather pleased about something I have said or done, or am likely to do, or that someone has said about me. I know that all things of concern to me are of equal concern to Corabelle, and though there may be nothing of it in actual words, I am made to feel that I am just as secure in my corner of Corabelle's heart as ever I was. I finish reading the letter with a very vivid remembrance of Corabelle's sympathy, a sense of loss in her absence, and a longing for the time when Corabelle herself may again be sitting on the sofa beside me and telling all the details her letter can but leave out.

A letter is a gift to a friend, and we must take care to fashion it

Sir, more than kisses, letters mingle souls. For, thus friends absent speak.

—JOHN DONNE
(1572–1632)

for her utmost enjoyment. I never write a letter without thinking of the way Corabelle's letters uplift my soul. And I have saved them all so that I may relive them again and again as often as I choose. Love in a letter endures forever. Take caution never to send your anger in words, for they too are not soon forgotten.

July 18, 1879
Darien, Georgia

Dearest Caroline,

I trust my letter has found you well and much recovered from our last visit to your lovely home. I am still dreaming of Sallie Anne's cooking and find myself chuckling every time I think of one of your amusing stories. Oh, how our visits make me long for the days when we were silly schoolgirls together!

Caroline, you will remember Dr. Benjamin Parham, the doctor in charge of the yellow fever quarantine station on Sapelo? We have just had a most enjoyable visit with him and his gracious and lovely wife, Louise. She remembered you fondly and told your alligator story which was so entertaining to those present, that it was referred to several times during the evening by our various guests.

I told all present of my fascination with Dr. Parham's beautiful, highly colored parrot which would sit unfettered on his handsome perch chattering incessantly in Spanish. Pedro, as he was called, had come off a Spanish ship and knew only two words in English, which every now and then he repeated in a most peremptory tone. They were "Four O'-Clock," which was the daily signal for the flag to be brought down to signal that no more ships could dock and the quarantine station was shut down for the night. Dr. Parham had us all laughing as he speculated what you might have taught the parrot to say. To my great surprise, upon his return to the island he sent Pedro to us as a gift along with a note explaining that his tenure of office was up and he and Louise were returning to Atlanta. James and I have delighted in taking walks around the grounds with Pedro chattering all the time in Spanish. Pedro had not been confined to a cage and has no interest in flying away, because, says James, my hat collection is simply too irresistible for exploring. (Particularly while on my head.) Our friends and neighbors adore him, especially the children. He has brought me much amusement and even made friends with the cat. I look forward to your next visit so that you may perhaps teach him one of your witty phrases.

Cousin Jamie visited last week and was eager to hear news of you. He said you had not written in quite some time and was concerned for you. I assured him you were as lively as ever. I am counting the days until your visit, dear precious Caroline!

I Remain,
Affectionately Yours,
Cousin Corabelle

The Thank-You Letter

A thank-you note or letter written in appreciation for gifts received and/or acts of kindness is an absolute must. There should never be a question in your mind as to whether or not it is called for, or deserved. It is rude not to acknowledge the kindness of others. The time, effort, and expense that went into the giving is certainly worthy of a kind response.

A thank-you letter should be sincere, expressing appreciation without excessive flattery. Clearly state what the thank-you is for. The tone should be pleasant. The letter should be short. The sincerity of the thank-you is emphasized by brevity. A prompt response (no later than ten days after receiving the gift) is always best, or if you were a house guest, no more than a week. Wedding gift thank-you letters are of course given a longer grace period, about two months. Below is a sample thank-you letter.

June 11, 1892

Dear Aunt Middle Mary,

You have that rare ability to select just the right gift. The puzzle you sent kept me up half the night! I'll get it yet. Thank you so much.

Fondly
Charles

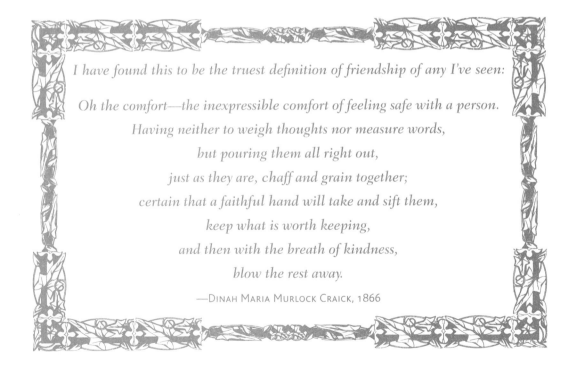

I have found this to be the truest definition of friendship of any I've seen:

Oh the comfort—the inexpressible comfort of feeling safe with a person.
Having neither to weigh thoughts nor measure words,
but pouring them all right out,
just as they are, chaff and grain together;
certain that a faithful hand will take and sift them,
keep what is worth keeping,
and then with the breath of kindness,
blow the rest away.

—DINAH MARIA MURLOCK CRAICK, 1866

The Condolence Letter

The first essential of a letter of sympathy is a tone of respect for the reader, who has just experienced one of life's harshest realities. A respectful mood is called for. After mentioning the deceased person's name, state your relationship, such as "Reinheardt, my childhood friend and schoolmate." Then make a complimentary statement such as "he was loved by all" or "he was always so friendly and unassuming." Recall a fond memory or relay some story that favors the deceased in a fitting way for the family to remember him by. If appropriate, offer to help the reader in some way. End your letter with a phrase such as, "Our thoughts and prayers are with you in this time of sorrow" or, "May the sympathy of those who care make the sorrow of your heart less difficult to bear." Condolence letters are so important to the grieving family. It is your duty to take the time and careful thought to write them.

My Dear Jackson,

We were all terribly upset to hear about your dear mother. She always brought us delicious treats during the holidays. The children were so fond of the entertaining stories she would tell as they gobbled their goodies. We will cherish those fond memories. What a lovely lady she was. She will be greatly missed.

My husband joins me in sending you our deepest sympathy and warmest wishes.

Affectionately yours,
Victoria Ashcroft
Wednesday

The Letter of Comfort

Letters written to those we love and care about when they experience the storms of life can be most comforting. Never underestimate the good such a letter can do for a hurting soul. Reaffirming that the suffering one is a strong, vital person along with encouragement to "stick it out" whatever the situation may be can make all the difference in someone's life. And your words can be relived over and over each time the recipient needs encouragement.

> "Finally brothers, whatever is true, whatever is noble, whatever is right, whatever is pure, whatever is lovely, whatever is admirable— if anything is excellent or praiseworthy— think about such things."
>
> —Philippians 4:8

Dear Children:

I write to tell you of the most extraordinary experience I encountered just this morning. I was going about my daily chores when something caught the corner of my eye. I looked toward the window and suddenly, as if on cue, a dozen yellow butterflies fluttered by. They popped like popcorn and danced a waltz. They flitted and flirted with the flowers. But they seemed to move in unison, as if they were one. And then as suddenly as they appeared, they were gone. So quickly, that for a moment, I wondered if I had imagined them. But it was such a perfectly splendid moment that it pierced my heart. I caught my breath and paused. I was in the midst of "the perfect moment." We all have hundreds of these in our lifetime. Moments when our present troubles are pushed far away as we behold a glimpse of something close to perfect. It may be a sleeping child, a phrase of music, or a shaft of sunlight on a snowy roof. Something that takes us out of ourselves, and for a brief moment, we are lifted out of the daily routine into untold realms of light and beauty. For an instant, we are in the presence of God, and nothing else matters. All of our worries and troubles fall away and we are aware of only the perfection that is before us. It is breathtaking and soul shaking. And then, the moment is gone. We are back on earth — but we are never the same.

We must learn to recognize these moments, for we all have them, though many of us no longer recognize them or know them by their proper name. The more we look for these moments, the more they seem to occur. And each time they occur, our souls are made deeper, our hearts —fuller. And we carry that fullness into the lives of the people we encounter.

Look for the perfect moments, dear children, and dwell on them. Drink them in like water. Seek them out and share them. And they will enrich and bless you and those you live with all the days of your life, for life is not measured by the breaths we take, but by the moments that take our breath away.

Love Always,
Big Mama

Mrs. Dunwoody's Indispensable Advice on Gift Giving

This advice may seem trite, but buying gifts for family and loved ones is something we do several times a year, regardless, so we might as well be good at it. Here are some things I've learned: Don't try to show off with an expensive gift. Gifts of your time and talent or trouble are worth much more and better appreciated and remembered. Bake a cake, take over a meal, or sit with the children. Anyone can go to the marketplace and spend a bundle for a useless item which only serves as one more thing to dust on cleaning day. It is always more meaningful (and, by the way, cheaper) to give from the heart.

Remember your children's teachers on holidays. Try homemade goodies or pampering items, such as scented hand soaps or lotions. Even better . . . a handwritten note expressing your appreciation of the effect the schoolteacher has had on your child's life.

Older folks would prefer a long letter and photographs or a special visit more than a wrapped gift.

Sometimes, surprise a friend with a thoughtful, small gift for no reason, a random act of love. ("Surcys" as Dear Mother called them.)

Make notes of things your friends and family admire. A trinket in the shop window, a book they mentioned, or even a color, fruit, or favorite day. Keep these "lists" of loved ones' favorites and delight them with a remembrance on their next birthday. "I knew you adored Wagner, so I bought you two tickets to his opera next Saturday." (I have found this habit to be so completely satisfying that I find myself making notes on people I hardly know!)

Give at least one gift anonymously every year. (The blessings will come back to you tenfold.) *Real* generosity is doing something nice for someone who'll never find out.

Record special events from your friends' and family members' lives and celebrate, or at least mention the event on the anniversary of their special day. ("It was a year ago today that you moved next door," and so forth.)

Don't "keep score" on gift giving. The true spirit of gift giving has no expectations attached. The point, after all, is to make someone happy, not to make yourself feel good. Never give with expectations or ulterior motives. And if someone asks you for something, don't judge whether or not she deserves it. Give it up freely and leave the rest to God. He should be the only scorekeeper.

Seven Gifts Which
Do Not Cost a Cent

1. *The gift of listening . . .* But you must *really* listen. No interrupting, no daydreaming, no planning your response. *Just listening.*

2. *The gift of affection . . .* With appropriate hugs, kisses, pats on the back, and handholds. These small actions demonstrate love in a powerful way.

3. *The gift of laughter . . .* Share amusing stories, humorous cartoons, and clippings from newspapers. Laughter establishes a bond between people and is one of the most effective medicines I know.

4. *The gift of a handwritten note . . .* Kind words change lives and last a lifetime.

5. *The gift of a compliment . . .* A simple kind and sincere remark can change how a person feels about himself.

6. *The gift of a favor . . .* Every week try to do at least one small act of kindness outside your family. (Acts of kindness are so hard to give away because they are almost always returned.)

7. *The gift of a cheerful disposition . . .* The easiest way to feel good is to extend a kind word to someone. Look him in the eye and speak kindly from the heart with sincerity.

A Little Common Sense

*The smallest act of kindness is worth more
than the grandest intention.*

When Someone Passes Over

Regardless of the fact that death is part of life, and we all are destined to that fate, it seems to paralyze us when we hear of one. But death is not time for hesitancy, panic, or indecision. This is a time to swoop down and fly into action, because without a doubt, the dear grieving family is beyond considering and dealing with the tedious details death demands. *You must be their everything.* You need to anticipate their every need and take care of it before they even have time to consider it. Refrain from the useless, "Let us know if there is anything we can do." Instead, *think* of something appropriate or helpful, and *do it!*

For the bereaved, true mourning consists of focusing on the life that has ended, as well as venting feelings of deprivation. While grief is fresh, every attempt to divert it only irritates, so possibly the most meaningful thing you could do would be to overlook the uncomfortable feelings you might experience regarding someone else's grief, and just sit and listen. No special words are needed, for there is nothing you can say to take away the loss. *Just sit and listen.* Be there. Sometimes "just listening" is the highest and best thing we can do.

A Plan of Action

Dear children, here in the South, we have this funeral business down to a fine art. Truly, I see no reason not to, since people always tend to die. And we all understand the importance of easing life's difficulties with rituals. The knowledge that there are set ways of facing these things emphasizes the repeating patterns of life, which is somewhat reassuring when they have been cruelly disrupted.

Upon entering the grieving family's home calmly and quietly, take charge like a general. Bring a well-thought-out plan and a few supplies. You must be strong and brave for the sake of the grieving family. Assume a matter-of-fact attitude—*"I am here to help for the duration, and we will get through this together . . ."* Take a close look at the family members. Ask yourself, "What little thing could I do to make this difficult time easier?" Assist with funeral plans? Take the children overnight? Tend to an errand or chore?

Instead of bringing food, think of the necessities. Some often overlooked but necessary items include: coffee and tea for guests, extra handkerchiefs and kitchen towels, serving pieces, trash receptacles, small plates and extra cups, fresh hand towels and hand soap for the powder room.

Assign a person to answer all incoming calls and inform the friends of the family of the funeral arrangements. Assign someone's son to run errands or deliver messages and someone else to tidy up the parlor and kitchen as needed. (Often I have sent my own maid for this purpose.) Ask a trusted friend to greet visitors at the door, and be ever mindful of how much the family can deal

"Always go to other people's funerals; otherwise, they won't come to yours."
—JUDGE DUNWOODY

From Mr. Denis Dandeneau's funeral,
I share this poem:

Do not stand at my grave and weep—
I am not there. I do not sleep.
I am a thousand winds that blow,
I am the diamond glints on snow.
I am the sunlight on ripened grain,
I am the gentle autumn rain.

When you awake in the morning's hush,
I am the swift uplifting rush
of quiet birds in circling flight.
I am the soft star-shine at night.
Do not stand at my grave and cry—
I am not there, I did not die.

—ANONYMOUS

with—guests, or not. Take care not to leave a frail or very distraught person alone. Make arrangements for a companion to be present morning, noon, and night.

Take every card that comes with flowers, write a description on the back of the card, clip it to a note card, and file it in a small box according to last name. Write down the names of all those who brought food and keep a "visitor's list" of all guests, so that after the funeral the family members may recall those who visited.

This is the way Southern women take care of each other, and I have often heard the appreciation from those on the receiving end of such attention to detail. When the grieving one is finally left alone and everyone has returned to their normal routines, the sting of death is fresh and sharp. These "records" of what family and friends did for one are a sweet comfort that cannot be fully realized until some time has passed.

After a week or two, the show of support is gone, and the grieving one is left alone to deal with the harsh reality of death, as inevitable as it may be. Make a special effort to call or visit *then*, instead of immediately after the death. Your visit will be more helpful and appreciated.

Writing a condolence letter to the grieving family can also be very comforting. Recall fond memories of the departed; share a

A Little Common Sense

It is selfish and rude to avoid acknowledging a death because you "didn't know what to say or do."

funny story or kind deed or words spoken. Help them remember happily and fondly the life of the one they have lost.

Many of us who lose loved ones "before their time" tend to focus on the day they died. A friend recently confided in me that her daughter had lived for eighteen vibrant years, and yet her husband had stayed focused on the day and unfortunate manner in which she had died, never appreciating or celebrating the many wonderful years he had with her. And truly, we must not grieve as an offering for a loved one, for that is not what they would want at all.

When I was an impressionable child of twelve, my grandfather died. I remember the preacher's words at his funeral. "If you believe in God Eternal, fret not, for you will be reunited with your loved one in the near future. But if you do not believe, you must come to the casket and say good-bye and pay your final respects, for this will be the last time you will see the man you know as Brother Frederick." Those words have served me well all my life, and I encourage you to offer them to anyone you know who is grieving.

"They say such lovely things about people at their funerals that it makes me quite sad to realize I will miss mine by just a few days."

—Aunt Middle Mary

Chapter Seven

Health and Beauty

Work on your <u>inner</u> beauty.
It counts for all eternity,
but your looks and youth will
soon wilt like a daylily.

Mrs. Dunwoody's Salutary Beauty Secrets

True beauty in a woman is reflected in her soul. It is the caring that she lovingly gives, the passion that she shows. And the beauty of such a woman only grows with the passing years.

☞ Exquisite neatness of person is inseparable from genteel breeding. It is a matter of principle as well as pride with the true lady not only to seem, but also to be, scrupulously clean. Untidiness not only puts friends to blush, but obscures the brightest talents as well.

☞ To dress well requires something more than a full purse and an attractive figure. It needs taste, good sense, and refinement. Dress may almost be classed as one of the fine arts.

☞ Ladies in making calls dress much more elegantly than for walking or shopping as a compliment to those visited.

☞ Buy handbags proportionate to your height and size.

☞ Your shoes, gloves, and handbag should be faultless and of the same color, or at least complement each other.

☞ Wear bright colors on gloomy days.

☞ *Always* wear black to funerals. Don't make a fashion statement. Make a compassion statement.

☞ Find out which colors look best and worst on you. Dress accordingly.

☞ Hair is a woman's shining glory, so don't neglect yours.

☞ Wearing shoes that hurt your feet will show in your face.

☞ To make eyelashes and eyebrows appear thicker and darker, dab a little petroleum jelly on them.

☞ Make your perfume scent last longer by mixing it with a dab of petroleum jelly.

☞ For itchiness around the eyes, use cucumber slices. They help relieve irritation.

☞ Of all things you may wear, your expression is the most important.

The Southern Belle's Beauty Secrets

☞ *For attractive lips, speak words of kindness.*

☞ *For lovely eyes, see the good in all people.*

☞ *For a slim figure, share your food with the hungry.*

☞ *For poise, walk with the knowledge that you will never walk alone, for the Lord is always by your side.*

☞ *Remember if you ever are in need of a helping hand, you will find one at the end of your arm.*

☞ *As you grow older, you will understand that you have two hands, one for helping yourself, and the second for helping others.*

—*GODEY'S LADY'S BOOK*, 1856 (SELECTED)

☞ Ladies never use profanity. These urges are best left to solitary gardening time.

☞ When in doubt, always . . . be poised and quiet.

Domestic Chemistry

Homemade Foot Powder

Make your own foot powder to absorb moisture and odor by mixing 1 ounce of powdered orrisroot with 3 ounces of zinc oxide and 6 ounces of talc. One batch should last 2 weeks if you use 1 teaspoon per shoe per day.

Beauty Prescription for Face and Neck

Blend the following ingredients until they form a paste: ½ cup of finely chopped cucumber, ½ cup of chopped avocado, 1 egg white, 2 teaspoons of powdered milk. Apply the mixture to your face in circular motions. Leave on for 30 minutes, rinse with clear, cold water, and pat dry.

Washing Brushes and Combs

Wash hairbrushes and combs by soaking them for a few minutes in a sink of water to which has been added a tablespoon of baking soda and a drop or two of bleach or other antiseptic. Swish a few times, then rinse.

A Dry Shampoo

You can make an easy homemade dry shampoo by mixing a tablespoon of baking soda into ½ cup of bran. Rub it into your hair when you don't have time for a wet shampoo, then brush it out.

R𝓍 for Dull Hair

Add the juice of ½ lemon or 2 tablespoons of cider vinegar to your rinse water.

Dry Hair Treatments

If you've got particularly dry hair and an itchy scalp, you might find relief from a rinse made with water to which a cup of vinegar has been added. Use the vinegar-water solution as your first rinse and then cool, clear water as a final rinse.

To soften hair, try a mayonnaise treatment. Rub in just enough to soak the hair thoroughly, and then comb it through. Let it remain on your hair for 30 minutes, then shampoo thoroughly and rinse with water that has a bit of lemon juice mixed in. Give your hair a final rinse with clear water or rinse with lemon water again. Your hair will feel luxurious and soft.

Face Freshener

Cider vinegar and lemon juice are inexpensive and handy astringents. Pour a few tablespoons of either into half a bowl of cool water and splash the mixture on your face after washing it. It will give your face a fresh, clean feeling.

To freshen up your face while traveling, carry a small bottle of witch hazel and some cotton balls. Then when your face feels grimy, dampen the cotton balls with the witch hazel and wipe it over your face and neck.

Lip Balm

½ cup almond oil

¼ cup cocoa butter

¼ cup coconut oil

1 tablespoon pure honey

2 ounces pure beeswax

1½ tablespoons vanilla

———

Heat the almond oil and stir in the cocoa butter and coconut oil. Stir in the honey and wax and test for firmness. Add a little more wax if needed. Then, stir in the vanilla. Pour into small, round containers. Allow to cool and harden before using.

For Facial Cleansing

———

Beat together for 3 full minutes the strained juice from ½ lemon and the white of 1 egg. Apply to your face, avoiding your eyes. Rinse after 30 minutes with cold water. Pat dry.

For Problem Skin

———

Mix 2 tablespoons of mineral water into 3 tablespoons of fuller's earth. Mix in 1 tablespoon of carrot juice, and add

"Safe guide to health: Keep the feet warm, the head cool, and the bowels open."

—Dr. Gideon Colfax Sr.

more fuller's earth as necessary to form a soft clay. Apply the clay to your face and leave it on for 20 minutes. Rinse with warm water and pat dry.

Dear Mother's Toothpaste Cream

Add 10 tablespoons of baking soda to 5 table-spoons of glycerine. Stir, then add 1 to 2 tea-spoons of peppermint flavoring. Store in an airtight jar.

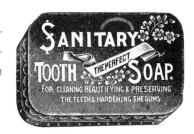

Geranium Perfume

A perfume may be made from the leaves of any sweet-smelling geraniums. The tincture, obtained by packing the leaves in a clean jelly jar and then filling it with alcohol, is easy to prepare. Let it stand for a few weeks before using. To strengthen the perfume, add a few more leaves.

Salubrious Medicinal Receipts

EDITOR'S NOTE: *Although some of these remedies are more than a hundred years old, they are still considered effective treatments, and in most cases much cheaper and safer than their modern-day equivalents.*

There is no point in which a woman needs more knowledge and discretion than in administering remedies for what seem slight attacks, which are *not supposed* to require the attention of a physician. Following, I offer my humble advice on such matters.

For Burns

A lifesaver: *Keep an aloe vera plant in the kitchen. When you burn or cut yourself, cut off one of the thick, rubbery leaves, squeeze out the juice, and rub the jellylike substance on your skin for quick, cooling relief. Also works well on irritated skin, diaper rash, or sunburn.*

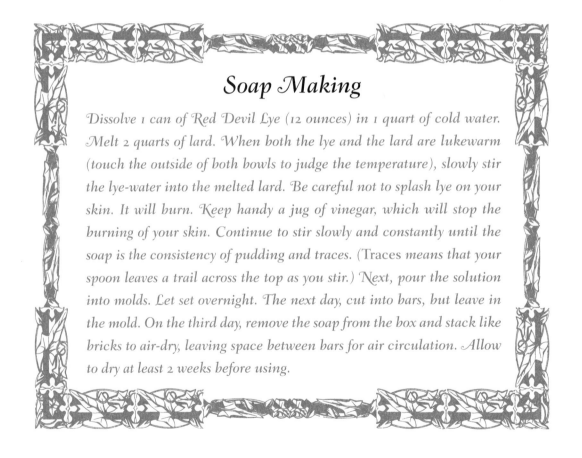

Soap Making

Dissolve 1 can of Red Devil Lye (12 ounces) in 1 quart of cold water. Melt 2 quarts of lard. When both the lye and the lard are lukewarm (touch the outside of both bowls to judge the temperature), slowly stir the lye-water into the melted lard. Be careful not to splash lye on your skin. It will burn. Keep handy a jug of vinegar, which will stop the burning of your skin. Continue to stir slowly and constantly until the soap is the consistency of pudding and traces. (Traces means that your spoon leaves a trail across the top as you stir.) Next, pour the solution into molds. Let set overnight. The next day, cut into bars, but leave in the mold. On the third day, remove the soap from the box and stack like bricks to air-dry, leaving space between bars for air circulation. Allow to dry at least 2 weeks before using.

Arthritis and Joint Pain

Take a teaspoon of molasses and red pepper three times a day. Externally, lay a cloth soaked in rubbing alcohol on the affected area; this is also good for mild headaches.

Constipation

Drink a tall glass of hot water before breakfast.

Cuts and Abrasions

If you are out in the woods and cut yourself badly, apply a spider's web to the wound. This will heal even more quickly if honey is applied to the wound. Bind it with a bit of moss. (Moss, you will remember, grows on the north side of a tree, in case you are lost.)

Eye Irritation or Mild Swelling

Elder leaves placed over the eyelids will offer relief from mild burning.

Fevers

Lemon balm is both cooling and refreshing; it is a mild fever reducer. For fever blisters, try applying cooled red clover tea on the affected area three times a day.

Headaches

Headaches are often a sign of a need for water. Sometimes a homemade seltzer will help; simply mix some baking soda and cold water with a splash of lime and drink before breakfast. Hot water with lemon is also beneficial.

Treatment for Inflamed Sore Throat

Gargle with an infusion of the herbs agrimony, myrrh, and/or sage. An infusion is prepared by adding 1 to 2 teaspoons of dried herb (or 2 to 4 teaspoons of fresh herb) to a cup of boiling water. Infuse for 10 minutes before straining. (If the herb is left too long, the infusion will become bitter.) The standard dosage is 1 cup three times a day. Never prepare the infusion more than 24 hours in advance.

Cough Suppressant

Mix apple cider vinegar and honey to taste in a small glass jar. Take a tablespoon as often as needed.

Natural Soother for Coughs

Infuse honey, cloves, and lemon in hot water as a natural remedy for coughs and sore throats. Sucking a whole clove will quiet tickles in the throat.

Heartburn

Add a tablespoon of raw apple cider vinegar to a glass of water and sip it while eating. Another remedy is to add 1 teaspoon of lemon juice to half a glass of water and drink.

Miss Olympia's Oatmeal Bath

Wonderful for sensitive skin!

Pour oatmeal into a square of cheesecloth. Close it tight with a rubber band and hang it under the water as the tub is filled. Once in the tub, use the cheesecloth bag of oat-

Dr. Colfax's Cure for Snoring

Known to have saved many a marriage!

Elevate the head of the bed by putting a brick or two under the two back legs. This raises the head and keeps the airway open. Do not put extra pillows under your head, for they will defeat the purpose.

If this method fails, sew a small rubber ball or marble into the middle of the back of the sleeping shirt. If the snorer rolls onto his back (the position most favorable for snoring), the ball will cause him to turn back to his side or stomach.

If neither of these methods is successful, it is suggested that the couple try separate sleeping quarters for the health of the marriage.

meal as a sponge. The oatmeal will soften and moisturize your skin. This is especially helpful in the treatment of chicken pox.

Treatment for Psoriasis

———

Epsom salts can relieve psoriasis. Make a paste with a little bit of water and pat it onto the tender spots. Or pour about 1 cup of the salts into a tub of lukewarm water and take a 30-minute soak.

Pepper Bath for the Feet

———

Have as much hot water as may be needed in a small tub; stir in mustard to make it sufficiently stimulating, or if pepper, boil a pod or two of pepper with the water. Put the

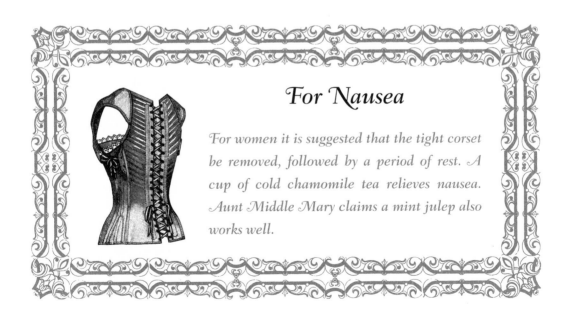

For Nausea

For women it is suggested that the tight corset be removed, followed by a period of rest. A cup of cold chamomile tea relieves nausea. Aunt Middle Mary claims a mint julep also works well.

patient's feet in the tub of water, and throw over the whole a blanket. Keep the water to the same temperature by adding a little warm water from time to time as may be needed. Rub dry with a coarse towel, and immediately cover up in bed.

For Depression

———

Take a bath with the leaves of rosemary and lavender. As you relax, sip a cup of chamomile tea and count your blessings.

For Insomnia

———

If troubled with wakefulness, follow these rules: Eat or drink nothing hearty after sunset; calm your mind before retiring (read or relax); go to bed at a regular hour; when you awake, rise and dress at once, no matter how early in the morning; and never sleep during the day. These five rules observed will ensure sleep.

Relief of Diarrhea

———

Red raspberry leaf tea works wonders and is gentle enough to give to babies.

To Settle the Stomach

———

Boil unrinsed white rice, then strain off the cooking liquid, cool, and drink.

To Stop Bleeding

——

Cayenne pepper stops bleeding; apply directly to minor cuts.

Wasp Stings

——

Apple cider vinegar applied to a wasp sting helps stop the pain. Also try a paste of baking soda and water.

Poison Oak

——

Milkweed plant can be used to relieve the itching of poison oak. Cut a piece of the stem and twist it back and forth until the juice oozes out. Apply directly to the itching area.

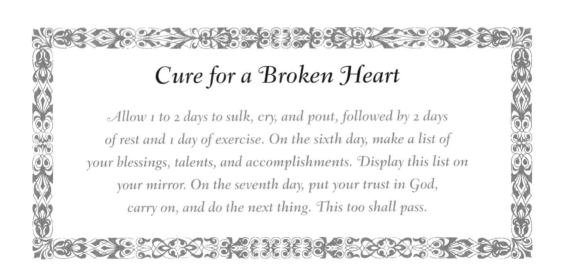

Cure for a Broken Heart

Allow 1 to 2 days to sulk, cry, and pout, followed by 2 days of rest and 1 day of exercise. On the sixth day, make a list of your blessings, talents, and accomplishments. Display this list on your mirror. On the seventh day, put your trust in God, carry on, and do the next thing. This too shall pass.

Cramps in the Leg

Stretch out the heel of the leg as far as possible, and at the same time, draw the toes as much as possible toward the leg. This is simple, but I have often known it to give immediate relief.

To Cure Hiccups

In all but one of my six children (Peter John), 1 spoonful of sugar swallowed immediately cured the hiccups. Some other remedies include holding your tongue out for as long as you're able, holding your breath, drinking soda water a gulp at a time while holding your breath, or swallowing a teaspoon of apple cider vinegar.

Herbal Teas

To make herb tea, heat 1 cup of water to boiling. Remove from the heat and add 1 to 3 teaspoons of dried herbs (or 1 to 3 tablespoons of fresh herbs). Allow to steep for several minutes. Sweeten with honey if desired. Use any combination of the following herbs and spices for the ailments present.

☞ *Fennel.* For stomachaches.

☞ *Ginger.* Reduces fever, and relieves vomiting.

☞ *Marjoram.* For fever, flu, and vomiting.

☞ *Nutmeg.* Aids in relieving pain, indigestion, and diarrhea.

Medicinal Notes

☞ *Whole cloves.* Good for digestion, upset stomach, and abdominal pain.

Weight Reduction

——

Plenty of water each day moisturizes the skin and releases stored fat. Eat your last meal of the day no later than 6:00 P.M. and have nothing but water until breakfast the next day. Do not skip meals; simply eat smaller portions. Take a long vigorous walk each day and find a hobby that keeps you moving.

To Extinguish Fire on a Person

Never rush into the air. When clothes catch on fire, extinguish by smothering; wrap up in wool if possible—a carpet, hearth rug, or anything within reach. If outside, do not run. Lie on the ground and roll until the fire is sufficiently smothered. Dr. Colfax told us of a young boy alone in his room, just in the act of retiring to bed, who discovered his nightclothes in a blaze by a spark from the fireplace. With admirable presence of mind, he leaped into bed, threw the covers over himself, smothered the flames, and thereby saved his own life!

If the chimney catches, so as to endanger the house, throw salt upon the fire; spread a wet blanket before the fireplace.

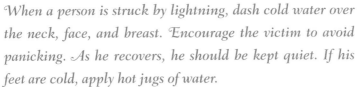

When Struck
by Lightning

When a person is struck by lightning, dash cold water over the neck, face, and breast. Encourage the victim to avoid panicking. As he recovers, he should be kept quiet. If his feet are cold, apply hot jugs of water.

Snakebites

Bind above the wound tightly. Give whiskey or some kind of strong drink. Beat an onion and an equal amount of tobacco cut up fine, the same quantity of salt; pour over half a tumblerful of boiling water, put it in a pot, and stew for 2 to 3 minutes. Cord above the wound as soon as possible after the wound is inflicted; apply the poultice. Repeat until the danger is over. This may also be used in the treatment of mad dog bites.

Care of a Sickroom

Through the years I cared for countless siblings, children, and friends as they became ill. Each patient has taught me valuable lessons in the care of the sick. When these details are properly attended to, I have found that both the patient and caretaker are very soon relieved of their respective roles as all returns to normal. Consider these instructions carefully.

Avoid loud talking or whispering; either extreme is painful to a sick person. This is absolute cruelty to the patient, for he will most likely think his complaint is the subject.

Make up the pillows, and turn them occasionally; arrange the bedclothes quietly; assist the patient to change his position; anticipate his wants in giving drinks, nourishments, et cetera, but at the same time, try to avoid being "fussy." A nervous person would prefer neglect to being persecuted by unnecessary attentions and needless questions.

Never take your seat on a sick person's bed unless requested to do so. Avoid shaking the bed. When a patient leaves his bed, open the sheets wide and throw the bedclothes back so as to thoroughly air the bed.

Darken the room to a mellow, twilight light, and ventilate the room so that a draft of air will blow, but not directly on the patient. If the patient is nervous, laboring under great excitement, or wishes to sleep, exclude all visitors. Sensible, considerate people will never take offense at this course.

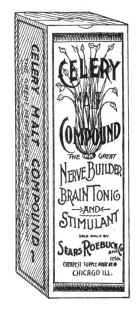

Wear slippers or cloth shoes; tread lightly. Dress should be of some soft material that does not rustle. Miss Nightingale denounces crinoline. Absolute quiet *is* necessary in the sickroom. Refrain from loud talking, and laughing, and prevent all discordant noises such as squeaking rocking chairs and reading the newspaper; the rattling of the paper in turning sometimes gives exquisite torture to a sick person.

Never let the patient be waked out of his first sleep by noise, never roused by anything like a surprise. Always sit so that the patient has you in view, and so that it is not necessary for him to turn in speaking to you. Never keep a patient standing; never speak to one while moving. Never lean on the sickbed. Above all, be calm and decisive with the patient, and prevent all noises overhead.

Let everything about the room be scrupulously neat. Bathe the hands and face of the patient upon waking in the morning and oftener, if needed. Change clothing and bedclothes frequently, and be sure they are perfectly dry. Follow the directions in giving medicine faithfully. When food is offered to a sick person, cover a tray with a white napkin. The china, glass, and flatware must be bright and clean, and a small quantity of food served, so as to be appetizing. Vary the dishes; the same things should not be offered every day. Never keep the patient waiting any length of time for nourishment; as far as possible, anticipate his wants. In some cases the patient will be too ill to eat more than a spoonful or two at a time, as his stomach may reject large supplies of food. In this instance, a spoonful of beef tea, or arrowroot and wine, or some other light, nourishing diet should be given every hour.

Never carry a sad, lugubrious face into a sickroom. Assume an attitude of confidence in your efforts, conveying to the patient that nothing but an absolute and total recovery is expected, regardless of the situation. Your attitude will be contagious to the patient, whether you realize it or not. "Trifles," it has been said, "make up the sum of human happiness or misery." This is certainly true of a sickroom. A great deal of pain and suffering is inflicted upon the sick by want of consideration, and not the wish or intention to be unkind.

Record of Family Illnesses

A record of your family's illnesses helps you remember what methods
of treatment are best, and how and when to expect recovery.

Patient	Date Began	Illness	Treatment	Date Recovered

Patient	Date Began	Illness	Treatment	Date Recovered

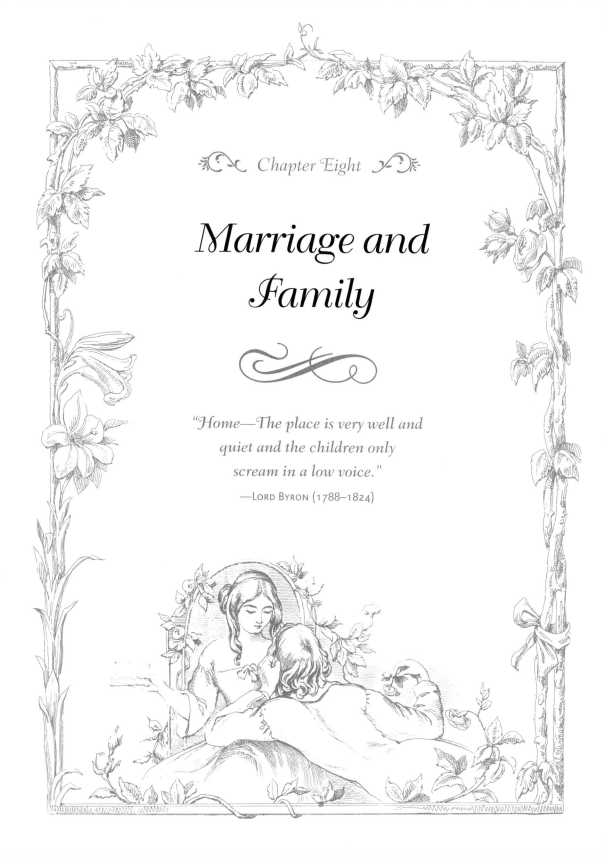

Chapter Eight

Marriage and
Family

"Home—The place is very well and
quiet and the children only
scream in a low voice."

—LORD BYRON (1788–1824)

Mrs. Dunwoody's List of Requirements for an Exceptional Spouse

Dear Mother used to say, "It's just as easy to fall in love with a rich man as it is a poor one." But I shall never dispense such useless advice to you, precious children. I have seen many an unhappy marriage where money was the motivation. Each of you would never be happy with mere material gain. Your hearts and souls are much deeper than that, and therefore will never be satisfied with anything material. Here are the qualities I have found most valuable in marriage (this list originated from my grandmother). And if you can find love for one who possesses these, you will be happy regardless of what life may throw your way.

1. *A sense of humor.* I'm sorry, precious children, but if your intended does not possess this, your mother will simply not permit the marriage.

2. *A positive outlook.* Ask yourself, "Does my love see the glass as half full or half empty?" Your days will be light and cheerful if the glass is half full. The Judge always surprised me with his ability to make the sweetest, most refreshing lemonade out of a bunch of sour old lemons. (There is a trick to it, you know.)

3. *A strong belief in God.* (Which covers such a multitude of shortcomings.) Enough said.

4. *Honesty.* If we cannot trust our spouse, then whom?

5. *Respect.* Don't overlook this one! Marriages can last without money, without children, without time spent alone to-

gether, without intimacy, and even without love, but no marriage can survive the loss of respect for one another. Try carefully to preserve it, for it can be the spark that ignites all others that have died and be the bridge for harmony and growth into a deeper, more meaningful relationship. Respect, like trust, it is a very hard thing to win back.

6. *Hard worker.* This goes for both men and women. Feeding a family requires a serious dedication to one's work. And raising a family is no Sunday picnic either!

7. *Compassion.* If your intended lacks the ability to empathize with you, even though you may not always agree, it

Prayer for a New Home

"O God, make the door of this house wide enough to receive all who need human love and fellowship, narrow enough to shut out all envy, pride and strife. Make its threshold smooth enough to be no stumbling block, but rugged and strong enough to turn back the tempter's power. God, make the door of this house the gateway to Thine eternal Kingdom, through Jesus Christ our Lord, Amen."

—SEEN INSIDE THE DOORWAY OF THE
OLD RECTORY AT CROWHURST,
SUSSEX, ENGLAND

will be painful and eventually erode away other positive aspects of the marriage.

8. *Forgiving.* You must always forgive. For we, all of us, are imperfect beings in an imperfect world. Forgiving one another is our only redemption.

9. *Generous.* By generous, I do not necessarily mean with money, but rather generosity of self and time. Generosity with emotions and actions. Is your love stingy with such things?

10. *Common sense.* It doesn't hurt to pick a man who knows not to dig a ditch in the rain. A commonsense man is more even tempered and easier to live with.

*The six most important words:
"I admit I made a mistake."*

The five most important words: "You did a good job."

The four most important words: "What is your opinion?"

The three most important words: "If you please."

The two most important words: "Thank you."

The one most important word: "We."

The least important word: "I."

For Lasting Happiness in Matrimony . . .

1. Realize that marriage is a lifelong commitment. It won't be easy every day, and some years won't be as good as others.

2. There are no two beings in the universe who have the same perspective. It should never be your intention in marriage to bring your spouse to *your* perspective. We should not strive to change our perspectives, *but rather to broaden them.* By praying for our spouse, about specific circumstances, we come to a broader perspective and appreciation of one another.

3. Each day speak kind words. Even if it is only, "Good morning, dear, did you sleep well?" A lifetime of kind words can add up to a happy marriage.

4. Understand that a true and lasting marriage is not a one-time commitment. It is a choice you make every day. It's the same challenge . . . and you cannot make a real commitment to anything unless you accept that it is a choice you make again and again, day after day, ongoing.

5. Always remember that being kind is more important than being right.

6. You *will* have disagreements. Accept that some things you will simply have to "agree to disagree on."

7. Learn to forgive and forget. To forgive is to set the prisoner free, and then discover the prisoner was you.

8. Love is in the details. You should know your spouse's favorite:

Color:

_____

Scent:

_____

Season:

_____

Flower:

_____

Place:

_____

Person:

_____

Book:

_____

Writer:

_____

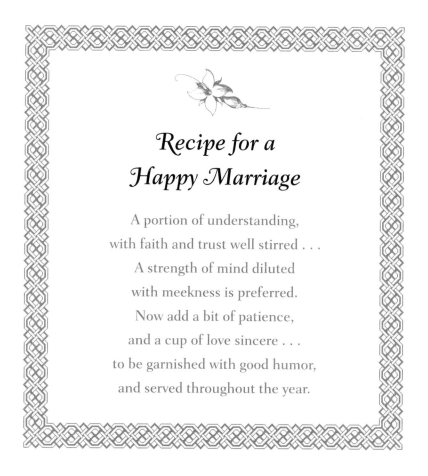

Recipe for a Happy Marriage

A portion of understanding,
with faith and trust well stirred . . .
A strength of mind diluted
with meekness is preferred.
Now add a bit of patience,
and a cup of love sincere . . .
to be garnished with good humor,
and served throughout the year.

A Little Common Sense

*Let the refining and improving of your own life keep you so busy
that you have little time to criticize others.*

Artist:

_____

Music:

_____

Poem:

_____

Food:

_____

9. Remember that it is the little things—a forgotten errand, a pair of unmentionables consistently left on the bathroom floor—that can become as irritating as a grain of sand in one's eye. When you live with another person, little things matter. Do something unselfish, unexpected, kind, and thoughtful for your spouse at *the very least* once a week.

10. A successful marriage is not finding the right person—it's *being* the right person.

A Little Common Sense

No husband has ever been shot while doing the dishes.

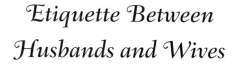

Etiquette Between Husbands and Wives

Let the rebuke be preceded by a kiss.

Do not require a request to be repeated.

Never should both be angry at the same time.

Never neglect the other, for all the world beside.

Let each strive to always accommodate the other.

Let the angry word be answered only with a kiss.

Bestow your warmest sympathies in each other's trials.

Make your criticism seldom, and in the most loving manner possible.

Make no display of the sacrifices you make for each other.

Never make a remark calculated to bring ridicule upon the other.

Never deceive; confidence, once lost, can never be wholly regained.

Always use the most gentle and loving words when addressing each other.

Let each study what pleasure can be bestowed upon the other during the day.

Always leave home with a tender good-bye and loving words.

—Hill's Manual for Social and Business Forms, 1888

A plaque bearing these rules hung on the wall of Dunwoody House for five decades.

Dunwoody House Rules for Small Children

Thou shalt not whine.

Always say the magic words, "please" and "thank you" and "I'm sorry."

Smile at everyone you meet.

Speak only kind words.

Put things back where they belong.

Ask permission.

Be helpful and kind to others.

A Little Common Sense

Your capacity for gratitude is directly related to your depth of happiness. Cultivate gratitude at all times.

Essential Manners
for Children

Good breeding consists of kindness and thoughtfulness toward others, as well as impeccable manners. Without them, you will be nobody, and with them, you may be anything. *So, too, you must teach your own children.*

Children should be taught from the time they are walking to:

☞ Meet and greet people politely.

☞ Be kind to others.

☞ Say "yes ma'am" and "no ma'am—or at least "yes" and "no," and that a grunt is not permissible.

☞ Always use the magic words "please" and "thank you."

☞ Display proper conduct in church and other public places.

☞ Respect their elders as well as all adults.

☞ Have proper manners and behavior at the table.

☞ Open doors for others.

☞ Remember that undesirable behavior will not be tolerated.

☞ Remember that there are unpleasant consequences for unwanted behavior.

☞ Remember that you always love *the child* if not always *the behavior.*

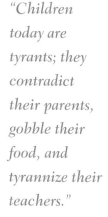

"Children today are tyrants; they contradict their parents, gobble their food, and tyrannize their teachers."

—SOCRATES
(470–399 B.C.)

Teaching Responsibility

Perhaps even more important than teaching children manners, is teaching them responsibility. Here are my ten rules, which I borrow from the third president of the United States, Mr. Thomas Jefferson.

1. Never put off till tomorrow what you can do today.

2. Never trouble another for what you can do yourself.

3. Never spend your money before you have it.

4. Never buy what you do not want because it is cheap.

5. Pride costs us more than hunger, thirst, and cold.

6. We never repent of having eaten too little.

7. Nothing is troublesome that we do willingly.

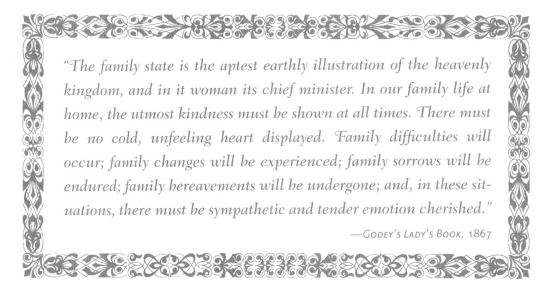

"The family state is the aptest earthly illustration of the heavenly kingdom, and in it woman its chief minister. In our family life at home, the utmost kindness must be shown at all times. There must be no cold, unfeeling heart displayed. Family difficulties will occur; family changes will be experienced; family sorrows will be endured; family bereavements will be undergone; and, in these situations, there must be sympathetic and tender emotion cherished."

—GODEY'S LADY'S BOOK, 1867

An Angry Wife and Mother's Silent Prayer

Lord, keep your arm around my shoulder and your hand over my mouth.

8. How much pain have cost us the evils which have never happened.

9. Take things always by their smooth handle.

10. When angry, count to ten before you speak; if very angry, a hundred.

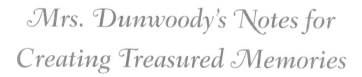
Mrs. Dunwoody's Notes for Creating Treasured Memories

Planning special time for the family holds untold treasure, for though we may not realize it in the early years, as we grow older these memories are among the most precious of our lives. Young children love rituals—it gives them a feeling of comfort and security as they anticipate the event. Create a short list of annual family traditions, such as:

☞ Prepare a child's favorite meal on his birthday and set the table in grand style.

The Golden Maxims for Family

The parental character must be highly respected.

Domestic order must be maintained.

The love of home must be fostered.

Sympathy under domestic trials must be expressed.

☞ Attend the same event each year on a holiday (such as the fireworks display on July 4).

☞ Celebrate the beginning of each season by decorating the house together and associating a certain meal with each season, serving it every year at the same time.

☞ Take an annual pilgrimage to somewhere special—the beach, the mountains, or even just your poor old mother's house.

☞ Select and decorate the Christmas tree on the same date each year. Serve the same meal each year after the decorating is done.

☞ Plant a family tree together. Also, plant one in the same year as your children's births. Name the tree after the child. Over time as he grows old with the tree, it will become a cherished memory for him.

☞ Create something together, such as a garden or crafts.

☞ Read an exciting adventure book aloud after dinner.

☞ Create a list of topics for discussions at dinner, such as, "Whom would you most like to meet?" or, "Describe your idea of a perfect day."

☞ Celebrate a family member's achievement together.

☞ Plan a family game night in the parlor after dinner.

The possibilities are endless, and the memories priceless. Your family will thrive and grow in love and laughter as you enjoy one of life's richest blessings.

A Little Common Sense

When hugging, never be the first to let go.

Chapter Nine

The Garden

The kiss of sun for pardon,
The song of the birds for mirth—
One is nearer God's Heart in a garden
Than anywhere else on earth.

—Dorothy Gurney

Planting Your Gardens

As you begin the planting season, may I suggest the following for your gardens.

Plant three rows of squash:

1. Squash gossip.
2. Squash criticism.
3. Squash indifference.

Plant three rows of peas:

1. **P**urity.
2. **P**atience.
3. **P**erseverance.

Plant six rows of lettuce:

1. Let us be unselfish and loyal.
2. Let us be faithful to duty.
3. Let us search the scriptures.
4. Let us not be weary in well-doing.
5. Let us be obedient in all things.
6. Let us love one another.

No garden is complete without turnips:

1. Turn up for church.
2. Turn up with a smile, even when things are difficult.

3. Turn up to always do your personal best.

4. Turn up for your family and friends as needed.

Flowers

I must admit, I would rather have fresh roses on my dining room table than sparkling diamonds around my neck! Fresh flowers and ornamental leaves have a magical effect on the decor of any room. A vase of flowers alone can transform the dreariness of any interior, and they are so inexpensive. I have found that autumn leaves, pussy willows, and cattails (these may be brightly colored) may be kept without water for as much as three months. Huckleberry, laurel, lemon, magnolia, or rhododendron leaves remain attractive for three to ten weeks.

Colorful, everlasting flowers may be used to add to an arrangement, or supplement arrangements, especially for winter decoration. Most of these are easily grown in the garden.

☞ *Ammobium alatum.* Winged everlasting—white.

☞ *Helichrysum bracteatum.* Strawflowers—various shades.

☞ *Gomphrena globosa.* Globe, amaranth—purple, white, rose.

☞ *Helipterum roseum.* Rose everlasting—pink.

☞ *Limonium latifolium.* Sea lavender—lavender.

☞ *Limonium sinuatum.* White or pink.

☞ *Lunaria annua.* Honesty—seedpods are silky, papery.

☞ *Physalis alkekengi.* Chinese-lantern—orange seedpods.

☞ *Xeranthemum annuum.* Immortelle—white, pink, lavender.

Arranging Flowers

My rule of thumb for height: For tall containers, use flowers twice the height of the container; for low containers, add the height plus the width. Cut the stem of the choice flower for the highest point in the arrangement. For a low design, substitute a line of length for the line of height. Have a design—a pattern. Start with a triangle in three dimensions. Place a second flower right and forward; a third flower to the left, opposite the second. Add more flowers of different lengths to fill. Let the buds and tendrils fall naturally, regardless of their height or position.

Select a focal point to which the eye should be drawn. Place your best blooms at this point. Lines should run toward this point. The focal point should be low in the arrangement. Open roses, gardenias, and camellias are some examples of good focal points. Consider container and flowers as one piece. Work your main design lines down to the mouth of the container. Leave some empty spaces toward the edges to avoid confusion in the design. Some basic patterns are a triangle, fan, column, crescent, oval, circle, and S curve. Avoid a square or zigzag line. The design should be in balance, preferably an asymmetrical balance. A figure in the container may balance the color in a flower, et cetera. Avoid mathematical precision.

To make the best use of cut flowers, particularly rare ones, place the vase before a mirror. This provides double effectiveness. Tall flowers may be set in a large vase on the floor, so that the blooms may be seen from above. Don't crowd flowers in a vase.

"Anyone with a lawn as large as a pocket hand-kerchief has within her reach a glimpse of heaven."

—DEAR MOTHER

Table centerpieces should be low so that guests may see each other across the table. My guests find it quite delightful to have a miniature arrangement at each place setting.

Flowers fall into two groups—round shapes (roses, carnations, tulips, daisies, zinnias, chrysanthemums) and elongated or spear shapes (gladiola, snapdragons, veronicas, hollyhocks, delphiniums). A good arrangement contains both. If one shape is not available, substitute leaves or ferns.

Sort colors first. Colors should be arranged light at the top, dark at the bottom. If you have various shades of one color, graduate them. But if only a few blooms are dark, use them as an accent, at the top or desired focal point. Apply the usual rules of color harmony.

Flowers should harmonize with each other and with the container and tablecloth; also, if possible, with the furnishings and style of the room itself.

I have found green linen thread to be most useful in tying stems and leaves. Broken stems may be braced with hairpins, wire, or toothpicks. Containers don't always have to be vases. I have used cups, teapots, mixing bowls, jars, pie plates, champagne flutes,

A Little Common Sense

Cut flowers will keep longer if you add a little salt to the water in which they stand and change it frequently. The salt slows the growth of decay-producing bacteria.

Perennials for the Cutting Garden

Aster   Baby's-breath   Bellflower

Black-eyed Susan   Blanketflower

Chrysanthemum   Delphinium   False sunflower

Flowering onion   Foxglove   Gay-feather

Globe thistle   Iris   Lavender   Meadow rue

Peony   Phlox   Purple coneflower

Sea holly   Speedwell

Tickseed   Yarrow

wineglasses, pewter, silver or copperware, a soup tureen, a wooden shoe, a bucket, a shell, an old jewelry box, an unused fireplace, and even an old umbrella stand. Use your imagination! Containers may be made of half a fruit shell, a hollowed-out cabbage, or even a ball of chicken wire. Stones, seashells, driftwood, seedpods, gourds, vegetables, fruit, and candles can also add to the display.

Experience the flowers as you work with them. Take notice of their exquisite color, texture, and smells, for they are truly one of God's most enjoyable gifts.

Dear Mother's Gardening Tips

☞ Want to know the secret to my beautiful African violets? Insert a few rusty nails into the soil around the violets. The blossoms will be larger, more profuse, and brighter in color.

☞ Beds of pansies will bloom more prolifically if you take a few moments to pinch out early buds. This encourages plants to bush out and, in the end, produce more flowers.

☞ When your hands are badly stained from gardening, add a teaspoon of sugar to the soapy lather you wash them in.

☞ In summer, water plants around noon, since plants will lose more water through their leaves in the peak temperatures of afternoon. During the winter, watering in the early morning is best because it offers a full day of rising temperatures, allowing top-watered greenery to dry off before dark. Never water at night, since this will encourage soggy soil around plant roots and lingering moisture on leaves—both invitations to disease.

☞ To keep dogs and cats out of the garden, steep 1 chopped garlic bulb and 1 tablespoon of cayenne pepper in 1 quart of water for 1 hour. Add 1 teaspoon of liquid soap to help the mixture stick to the plants. Strain the portion you need into a watering can and sprinkle it onto plant leaves. The rest will remain potent for several weeks if kept cool in a covered jar.

☞ Slugs and snails hate wood ashes. Sprinkle ashes around flower and vegetable plants. The ashes are a good source of potassium, unlocking nutrients so that the plants can absorb them. Ashes also prevent radish maggots: Sprinkle ashes over seeds before covering with soil.

☞ Plant a few sprigs of dill near your tomato plants to prevent tomato worms.

☞ Marigolds will prevent rodents.

☞ Prevent mosquitoes from breeding in rain barrels by floating 1 tablespoon of olive oil on the water's surface.

The Language of Flowers

In days of old, flowers were not given merely as a thing of beauty, but rather as a way of expressing feelings. If a man gave a bouquet of honeysuckle and apple blossoms, his secret message was, "You are preferred, and I am devoted to thee." This is known as "the language of flowers" and has become universal.

☞ *Acacia.* Friendship.

☞ *Almond Blossom.* Encouragement.

☞ *Aloe.* Grief.

☞ *Anemone.* Soul of goodness.

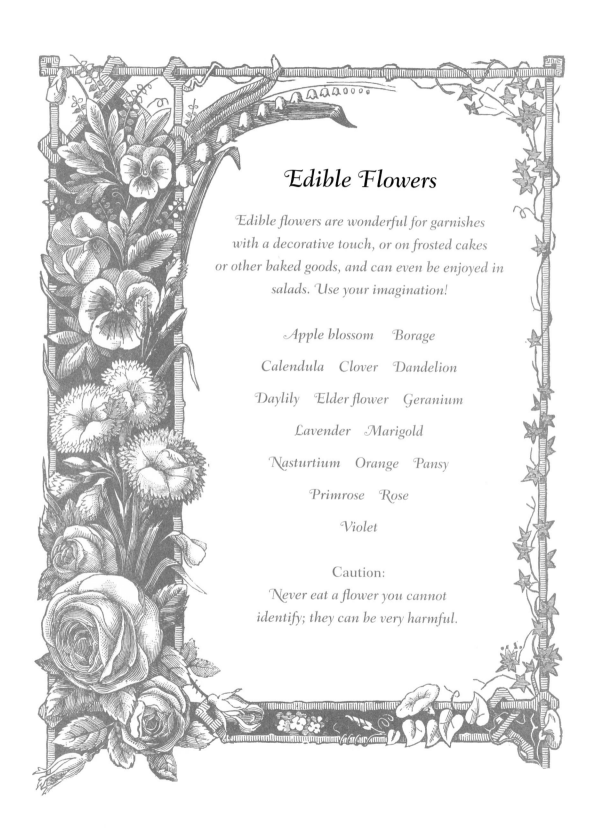

Edible Flowers

Edible flowers are wonderful for garnishes with a decorative touch, or on frosted cakes or other baked goods, and can even be enjoyed in salads. Use your imagination!

Apple blossom   Borage

Calendula   Clover   Dandelion

Daylily   Elder flower   Geranium

Lavender   Marigold

Nasturtium   Orange   Pansy

Primrose   Rose

Violet

Caution:
Never eat a flower you cannot identify; they can be very harmful.

☞ *Apple Blossom.* You are preferred.

☞ *Arbutus.* I love but thee.

☞ *Aster.* Always gay.

☞ *Balm.* Sympathy.

☞ *Begonia.* Steadfast.

☞ *Blackthorn.* Courage under trials.

☞ *Bluebell.* True and tender.

☞ *Buttercup.* Homeliness.

☞ *Camellia.* Beautiful, but cold.

☞ *Carnation, white.* Purity.

☞ *Carnation, red.* My heart is broken.

☞ *Chrysanthemum.* Hope springs eternal.

☞ *Clematis.* Beautiful thoughts.

☞ *Clover, white.* Think of me.

☞ *Clover, red.* Sweetness.

☞ *Columbine.* Bound to win.

☞ *Cornelian.* Content.

☞ *Crocus.* Ever glad.

☞ *Daffodil.* Welcome.

☞ *Dahlia.* Gracious.

☞ *Daisy.* Innocence.

☞ *Fern.* Sincerity.

☞ *Forget-me-not.* Forget me not.

☞ *Foxglove.* Deceitful.

☞ *Fuchsia.* Fickleness.

☞ *Gentian.* Hope.

☞ *Geranium.* Warm regard.

☞ *Hawthorn.* Courage in adversity.

☞ *Heather.* I am lonely.

☞ *Holly.* Rejoice together.

☞ *Honeysuckle.* Devotion.

☞ *Hyacinth.* Hard fate.

☞ *Iris.* Have faith in me.

☞ *Ivy.* I cling.

☞ *Jasmine.* Friends only.

☞ *Laurel.* Triumph.

☞ *Lavender.* Sweets to the sweet.

☞ *Lilac.* Unadorned beauty.

☞ *Lily.* Austere purity.

☞ *Lily-of-the-valley.* Doubly dear.

☞ *Magnolia.* Magnanimity.

☞ *Marigold.* Honesty.

☞ *Mignonette.* Undiluted pleasure.

☞ *Nasturtium.* Optimism.

☞ *Olive.* Peace.

☞ *Orange Blossom.* Happiness in marriage.

☞ *Pansy.* Thoughts are with you.

☞ *Petunia.* I believe in thee.

☞ *Pimpernel.* Consolation.

☞ *Poppy.* Forgetfulness.

☞ *Primrose.* Do not be bashful.

☞ *Rose, red.* Love.

☞ *Rose, white.* Worthy of love.

☞ *Rose, yellow.* Why waneth love?

☞ *Rosemary.* Remembrance.

☞ *Snowdrop.* Goodness unalloyed.

☞ *Sweet Pea.* I long for thee.

☞ *Sweet William.* Pleasant dreams.

☞ *Tulip.* Unrequited love.

☞ *Verbena.* You have my confidence.

☞ *Violet.* Modesty.

☞ *White Heather.* Good luck.

Houseplants

Nearly as lovely and engaging as fresh flowers in the home, are houseplants. There are several species of foliage plants, such as English ivy and a few flowering plants, that will do well in a north window, or even away from a window if the room is light. In general, east windows that receive full sun until noon are probably best suited for potted plants. South windows get the sun for a

Dear Mother's Flower Garden

Leaves from
The Language of Flowers

Angelica	*Clematis*	*Jasmine*
Inspiration	Beautiful thoughts	Friends only
Camomile	*Holly*	*Sweet Violet*
Energy in adversity	Rejoice together	Modesty
Cedar	*Honeysuckle*	*Water Lily*
Strength	Devotion	Purity of heart

longer time than east windows, but often the temperature is high enough at midday to interfere with plant growth. West windows are seldom so satisfactory as east or south, probably because the temperature fluctuates widely between midafternoon and night.

To Begin Your Vegetable Garden

Dear Mother gave me these instructions when I took up home-keeping, and they have served me beautifully. This garden, planted as Mother suggested, can feed a family of four for one summer with a little extra for giving away or preserving. (Eat what you can and can what you can't.)

A good size for a beginner vegetable garden is 10 feet by 16 feet. Make your garden eleven rows of 10 feet each. Ideally the rows should run north and south to take full advantage of the sun.

I suggest the following crops due to their ease in growing. Later, as you become more experienced with your vegetable garden, you may wish to add other varieties.

Row

1   *Zucchinis (4 plants)*

2   *Tomatoes (5 plants)*

3   *Peppers (6 plants)*

4   *Cabbage*

5   *Bush beans*

6   *Lettuce*

7   *Beets*

8   *Carrots*

9   *Chard*

10 *Radishes*

11 *Marigolds (to discourage rabbits)*

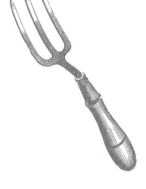

The Butterfly Garden

Butterfly gardening involves planning your garden to attract, retain, and encourage butterfly populations. Over the years, my many guests have always loved my butterfly garden. By putting window boxes outside the downstairs windows, even the feeblest of guests have been able to enjoy viewing the butterflies as they fluttered against the window, anxious to extract nectar from a nearby flower. Here are a few hints to begin a successful butterfly garden of your own:

☞ Butterflies go through several stages of life which all need to have a place in your garden. First the egg laying, then the hungry caterpillar, next the chrysalis, and finally the butterfly itself all need to have certain environments provided.

☞ Plants and flowers, of course, are the key to attracting butterflies to your garden. There are hundreds of different specimens of butterflies, and each is attracted to certain kinds of plants, so you may want to do a little research for the best plants for your area. You should select a variety of nectar-producing plants with the aim of providing flowers in bloom throughout the season. This will entice a continuous succession of new, delightful, and surprising guests to the yard (not to mention the glorious butterflies). It is especially important to have flowers in mid- to late summer, when butterflies are most active. Flowers with multiple florets that produce abundant nectar are ideal. Annuals are wonderful butterfly plants because they bloom continuously through the season, providing a steady supply of nectar. Perennial plants such as cornflower, lilac, butterfly weed, and aster are visited regularly by butterflies. Others I have had success with include: bee balm, dahlia, geranium, hibiscus, impatiens, marigold, herbs in the mint family, phlox, salvia, snapdragon, yarrow, yellow sage, and zinnia. Also try heirloom-type plants such as cosmos, dame's-rocket, hollyhock, honeysuckle, joe-pye weed, nasturtium, sweet pea, pink, and sweet William.

☞ If you have a supposedly good butterfly plant that is not attracting butterflies, it may be that this plant is not the preferred larval food of the butterflies in your particular area. This is why I suggest a little research before you begin.

☞ Make sure you have plenty of leaves for the caterpillar stage. Caterpillars are particularly fond of milkweed, nettles, dill, parsley, Queen-Anne's-lace, carrots, fennel, and hackberry.

☞ Since butterflies are cold blooded, they will avoid shady areas. Pick a sunny spot for planting your garden. Also try to plant out of the wind. A butterfly's wings are very fragile, and for this reason they avoid fighting wind gusts. They prefer to feed and lay eggs in somewhat sheltered areas. Planting near a hedge of lilacs, butterfly bushes, or viburnums will provide a good nighttime shelter for the butterflies.

☞ Add a few good-size rocks among your flowers. Butterflies enjoy sunbathing on them.

☞ Placing a bowl of wet sand or creating a mud puddle in your garden will encourage butterfly puddling. Butterflies do not drink from open water. They are drawn to moisture rather than water.

☞ Rotting fruit such as bananas and apples will attract butterflies.

Planting an Herb Garden

I have enjoyed my herb garden perhaps more than any other of my gardens. There is something so satisfying about dressing up a plain old dish of potatoes with fresh-grown herbs from one's own garden! Here are my favorites:

☞ *Basil.* A must with tomatoes! Also good with peas, squash, lamb, fish, eggs, tossed salad, cheese, duck, and potatoes.

☞ *Chives.* A wonderful light onion flavor good with meats, cheeses, vegetables, and salads.

☞ *Dill.* Good with fish dishes, cream and cottage cheese, potatoes, vegetables, and tomatoes.

☞ *Mint.* Wonderful in tea, fruit juices, mint juleps, jellies, candies, frosting, cakes, pies, lamb, and ice cream.

☞ *Oregano.* Tomato sauces, pork and veal dishes.

☞ *Parsley.* Good with all meats and vegetables. Good as a garnish and breath freshener, and cures an upset stomach.

☞ *Rosemary.* Good in veal and lamb roasts, potatoes, cauliflower, fish, and duck.

☞ *Sage.* Use in stuffings, pork roasts, sausages, and poultry.

☞ *Tarragon.* Good in fish sauces, egg and cheese dishes, pickles, for flavoring vinegar, and in sauces for meats and vegetables.

☞ *Thyme.* Good in soups, clam chowders, stuffings, beef, lamb, veal, and pork dishes, oysters, eggs, and cheese.

An easy way to get started is to turn an old wooden ladder into a small herb garden. This makes it easy because it defines the area you will be working in and relieves you of having to worry too much about "garden design." Lay the ladder flat on the ground. Fill with topsoil and manure and plant a different herb in between each rung. In laying out the plants, here are some considerations:

☞ Sage grows quite tall, and may mark the tallest part of your garden's elevation.

☞ Creeping rosemary, thyme, oregano, and marjoram are low-growing plants which may ooze over the edges of the ladder garden and soften it somewhat.

☞ In between will be somewhat bushy upright basil, rosemary, tarragon, and ferny dill.

☞ If you don't care for the "bare" look in the beginning, plant the edible annual lemon gem marigolds. They are cheerful and pretty, and their tiny flowers are tasty sprinkled on salads.

☞ Mint can be very invasive and prefers "wet feet." So it would perhaps be happiest outside of the ladder in the rudest and dampest section of your yard.

☞ Ideally, the herb garden can be planted in autumn. Snowfall creates a blanket of protection for the herbs. In fact, many herbs will continue to grow beneath the snow.

☞ Parsley serves as an ideal border in a traditional four-square herb garden. The garden is equally divided into four sections in a + or x design. Wood or plantings (such as parsley) can be used to divide the sections.

☞ To protect your herbs from winter wind damage, plant them on the south or west side of the house. Most herb gardens do best in full sun, but many can survive on as little as six hours per day.

☞ Cut, nip, and prune herbs regularly to stimulate continued growth. Cut chives 1 inch from the base of the plant.

☞ Paper sacks make great dryers for home-grown herbs. Put herb leaves in a paper sack and tie the top or fold it over twice. Don't fill the bag more than half full. Note the contents on the front and store in a dry place such as your pantry, away from direct sunlight. Shake the herb bag daily. Herbs should be completely dry in a week. Remove and store dried herbs in a dry, airtight container. Glass jars with lids work well.

☞ Don't throw out old window screens. They are perfect for drying herbs on. Lay a second screen on top of the first one containing the herbs to keep them from blowing away.

Gardening Notes

Gardening Notes

Chapter Ten

Final Remarks

Work and love,
—these are the basics.
Without them
there is neurosis.

—THEODOR REIK

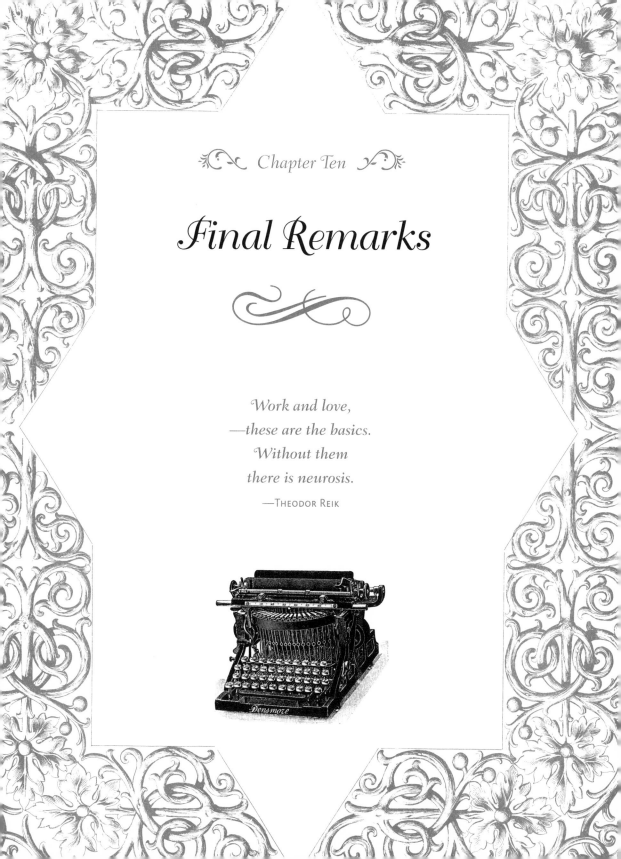

Finding Your Life's Work

There is for each of us a place of *perfect self-expression*. It is a place in life that only we can fill, no one else will do, and we are happiest when we are in the center of it. Many of us have no idea what this perfect self-expression is, or we doubt that we are worthy of such a blessing. I believe that each person has some talent which is unfulfilled in some hidden area of his being—a talent waiting to be expressed or developed, even though many live their entire lives unaware of it. But it is there, for each of us, designed by God to be our life's work. This "life's work" will be so completely absorbing and satisfying that it will seem more like play. Your soul will long for it.

"Neglect not the gift that is in thee."

—1 TIMOTHY 4:14

We can never depend on people or things to make us happy. They only temporarily shelve our dissatisfaction. Eventually, the nagging, God-size hole inside of us returns begging to be filled. Man has tried to fill it with fame, fortune, power, immoral conduct, and indulgent behavior. As it has been written, "Even the man who knocks on the door of a brothel is trying to fill the emptiness in his soul, though he knows it not." The hole remains until we discover our God-given treasure. For nothing can fill that which is meant for God. Do you imagine that the same Spirit who created the countless wonders and miracles of this world created you *without a specific purpose?*

We must ask God to manifest His plan for our life. As we consistently ask Him, God will release the genius within each of us. He will guide us to our destiny if we but ask for it and stay ever watchful for new experiences and opportunities. When we realize that there is an invincible power that protects us and all that we love, and brings to us every righteous desire of our hearts, we can relax and all things fall into place.

Dear children: *We are not here merely to make a living, or exist for our own amusement.* We are here in order to enrich the world and lives of others, and you impoverish yourself if you forget the errand. And poverty of purpose, my dears, is far worse than poverty of purse.

Some people may never know or realize their perfect self-expression. They have wandered far beyond God's plan for their lives. They are living far below their possibilities because they are continually handing over their individuality to others. Do you want to be a power in this world? Then be yourself. Follow your heart. Be true to the highest that is within your soul. Ask the Christ within to release your perfect self-expression. As Matthew Arnold said, "Resolve to be thyself; and know that he who finds himself, loses his misery."

Man's ultimate freedom comes through fulfilling his destiny, for man is happy only as he finds a work worth doing—and does it well.

Happiness is to be found along the way, not at the end of the road, for then the journey is over; it is too late. Today, this hour, *this very minute,* is the moment for each of us to sense that life is wonderful, even with all of its trials and tribulations, and perhaps more interesting because of them. The unthankful heart discovers no mercies; but the thankful heart will find in every hour, some heavenly blessings. Consider carefully how you will look at life—for it is like that. All that we are is the result of what we have thought. The mind is everything, and what we think, we become.

Mrs. Dunwoody's Guide to Living Beautifully

☞ Realize that each new day is a gift from God. Treat it as such.

☞ Focus on life's blessings, as this is continuously uplifting, and affects who you are as a person.

☞ Develop a keen appreciation for the little luxuries in your daily life—the smell of coffee in the morning, the songbirds outside your window, a loved one's crooked smile. Seek out these "blessings" and take time each day to notice and savor them. Pay attention to your life.

☞ Create a home you love to live in.

☞ Spend some time outdoors. Nature heals and replenishes the soul.

☞ Do something kind for someone at least every week; aim for every day. Do a good deed anonymously. You will find, in time, that the more you give, the more is given back to you.

☞ Everything in life is a choice. Realize that as you live your life, each moment you are either adding to or taking from the quality of your life. You are either creating and enjoying, or dying and destroying. There is no "standing still," for that is time wasted and therefore takes away from your life. The choice for your life is up to you.

☞ Strive to become the best version of yourself.

☞ To awaken mentally and become passionate about something, find the thing that moves your heart and stirs your soul. Persevere, for passion is a necessity for a beautiful life.

☞ Create something, whether it is a family, a meal, a painting, or a daydream.

☞ Never stop learning, through books, people, travel, and experiences.

☞ Listen to and enjoy another's company often.

☞ Focus on your love of beauty.

☞ Treat yourself well. Use the fine china for your cup of tea.

☞ Cultivate gratitude in all things and circumstances. Search for the good in all.

☞ Speak only kind words.

☞ Laugh every day.

☞ Give continual thanks and praise to your Creator, and ask Him to guide your heart and soul.

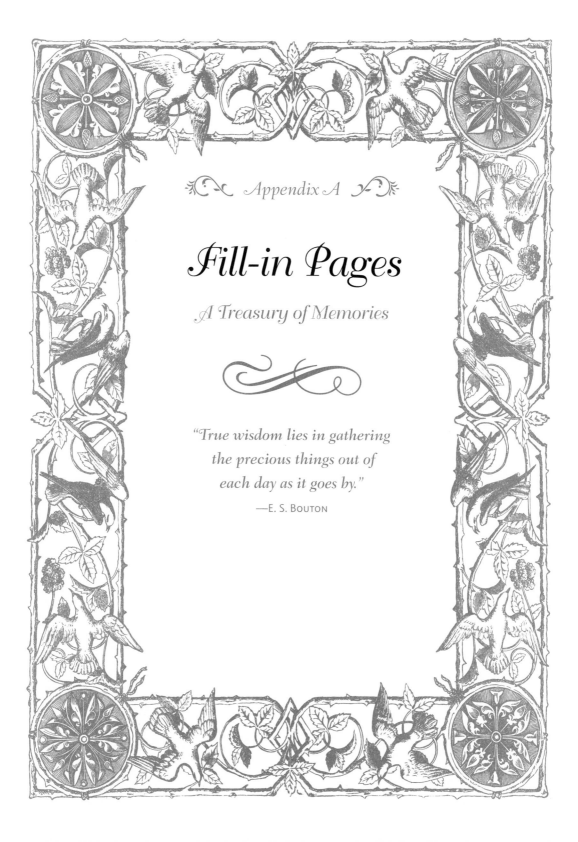

Appendix A

Fill-in Pages

A Treasury of Memories

"True wisdom lies in gathering
the precious things out of
each day as it goes by."
—E. S. BOUTON

Begin your own notebook celebrating life and wisdom to pass down to the next generation. On the next few pages are some sample records to get you started.

A family record is more than names, dates, and places. It is about people—what they did, why, and how. All of us know something of our living relatives. We enjoy telling stories about their achievements and exploits, and we certainly have a fondness for the enduring characters who pepper our families. Yet our knowledge of our families often does not go beyond those members we actually know. Few of us have been lucky enough to know our great-grandparents, for example. One of the most common ways of learning about ourselves is by word of mouth: the so-called oral tradition. Often we do not appreciate its worth until we are too old to question older family members, for they have passed on, and with them the library of information they possessed. Thus, if you want to start finding out more about your family, the place to start is with your relatives.

Consider that each of us has four grandparents, eight great-grandparents, sixteen great-great-grandparents, and thirty-two great-great-great-grandparents. With a conservative average of twenty-five years between each generation, this means that during the past five hundred years, there were 1,048,576 persons—all contributing to the production of you! We must always pay respect to our roots. Genealogical research helps us to learn about ourselves and recognize and appreciate the wonderful individuality that all persons possess. This makes us, like the snowflakes, no two alike.

This book provides you the opportunity to gather together in one place all the interesting and unusual aspects of your family's history. When complete, it will be a storehouse of treasured information, achievements, and memories—a permanent record of your family which is unique and unlike any other, just waiting to be discovered and cherished by your very own descendants. And so the circle of life continues.

Husband's Family Tree

Name _____

Birthplace _____ Date _____

Brothers and Sisters _____

Parents

Father

Name _____

Birthplace _____ Date _____

Mother

Name _____

Birthplace _____ Date _____

Grandparents

Paternal

Grandfather _____

Birthplace _____ Date _____

Grandmother _____

Birthplace _____ Date _____

Maternal

Grandfather _____

Birthplace _____ Date _____

Grandmother _____

Birthplace _____ Date _____

Great-Grandparents

Paternal

Grandfather's Father _____

Birthplace _____ Date _____

Grandfather's Mother _____

Birthplace _____ Date _____

Grandmother's Father _____

Birthplace _____ Date _____

Grandmother's Mother _____

Birthplace _____ Date _____

Maternal

Grandfather's Father _____

Birthplace _____ Date _____

Grandfather's Mother _____

Birthplace _____ Date _____

Grandmother's Father _____

Birthplace _____ Date _____

Grandmother's Mother _____

Birthplace _____ Date _____

Wife's Family Tree

Name

Birthplace   Date

Brothers and Sisters

Parents

Father

Name

Birthplace   Date

Mother

Name

Birthplace   Date

Grandparents

Paternal

Grandfather

Birthplace   Date

Grandmother

Birthplace   Date

Maternal

Grandfather

Birthplace   Date

Grandmother

Birthplace   Date

Great-Grandparents

Paternal

Grandfather's Father

Birthplace   Date

Grandfather's Mother

Birthplace   Date

Grandmother's Father

Birthplace   Date

Grandmother's Mother

Birthplace   Date

Maternal

Grandfather's Father

Birthplace   Date

Grandfather's Mother

Birthplace   Date

Grandmother's Father

Birthplace   Date

Grandmother's Mother

Birthplace   Date

Special and Memorable Events

*"Some memories are realities, and are better than anything
that can ever happen to one again."*

—WILLA CATHER

Event	Place	Date

Marriages

"Two souls and one thought,
two hearts and one pulse."

—HALEN

Bride	Groom	Place	Date

Fill-in Pages: A Treasury of Memories

Births

Name	Born To	Date

Deaths

Name	Date

Oral Family History

As told by . . .

_____

_____

_____

_____

_____

_____

_____

_____

_____

_____

_____

_____

_____

_____

_____

_____

_____

_____

_____

_____

_____

_____

_____

_____

_____

_____

Favorite Family Stories

Favorite Family Recipes

_____

_____

_____

_____

_____

_____

_____

_____

_____

_____

_____

_____

_____

_____

_____

_____

_____

_____

_____

_____

_____

_____

_____

Out of the Mouth of Babes

Cute sayings or doings of children.

_____

_____

_____

_____

_____

_____

_____

_____

_____

_____

_____

_____

_____

_____

_____

_____

_____

_____

_____

_____

Notes

Nothing is a waste which makes a fond memory.

Notes (continued)

Notes (continued)

_____

_____

_____

_____

_____

_____

_____

_____

_____

_____

_____

_____

_____

_____

_____

_____

_____

_____

_____

_____

_____

_____

_____

_____

_____

Notes (continued)

Fill-in Pages: A Treasury of Memories

Notes (continued)

Notes *(continued)*

Fill-in Pages: A Treasury of Memories

Notes *(continued)*

Notes (continued)

Fill-in Pages: A Treasury of Memories

"When trouble or heartaches come . . . trust in God and do the next thing."

—CAROLINE ANNE WYLLY DUNWOODY
(1841–1925)

Mama's Mama on a winter's day,
Milked the cows and fed them hay,
Slopped the hogs, saddled the mule,
And got the children off to school.
Did the washing, mopped the floors,
Washed the windows and did some chores.
Cooked a dish of home-dried fruit,
Pressed her husband's Sunday suit,
Swept the parlor, made the bed,
Baked a dozen loaves of bread.
Split some wood and lugged it in,
Enough to fill the kitchen bin,
Cleaned the lamps and put in oil,
Stewed some apples she thought might spoil,
Churned the butter, baked a cake,
Then exclaimed, "For mercy's sake,
The cows have got out of the pen!"
Went out and chased them in again,
Gathered the eggs and locked the stable,
Returned to the house and set the table,
Cooked a supper that was delicious,
And afterwards washed all the dishes,
Fed the cat, sprinkled the clothes,
Mended a basket full of hose,
Then opened the organ and began to play,
"When You Come to the End of a Perfect Day."

—ANONYMOUS

Useful
Information

Table of Measures

Apothecaries

    1 scruple = 20 grains
    1 dram = 3 scruples
    1 ounce = 8 drams
    1 pound = 12 ounces

Avoirdupois

    1 ounce = 16 drams
    1 pound = 16 ounces
    1 hundredweight = 100 pounds
    1 ton = 2,000 pounds
    1 long ton = 2,240 pounds

Dry Measure

    2 pints = 1 quart
    4 quarts = 1 gallon
    2 gallons = 1 peck
    4 pecks = 1 bushel

Liquid Measure

    4 gills = 1 pint
    2 pints = 1 quart
    4 quarts = 1 gallon
    63 gallons = 1 hogshead
    2 hogsheads = 1 pipe or butt
    2 pipes = 1 tun

Linear Measure

1 foot = 12 inches
1 yard = 3 feet
1 rod = 5½ yards
1 mile = 320 rods
1 mile = 1,760 yards
1 mile = 5,280 feet
1 international nautical mile = 6,076.1155 feet
1 knot = 1 nautical mile per hour
1 furlong = ⅛ mile
1 furlong = 660 feet
1 furlong = 220 yards
1 league = 3 miles
24 furlongs = 3 miles
1 fathom = 2 yards
1 chain = 100 links
100 links = 22 yards
1 link = 7.92 inches
1 hand = 4 inches
1 span = 9 inches

Square Measure

1 square foot = 144 inches
1 square yard = 9 square feet
1 square rod = 30¼ square yards = 272¼ square feet
1 acre = 160 square rods = 43,560 square feet
1 square mile = 640 acres = 102,400 square rods
1 square rod = 625 square links
1 square chain = 16 square rods
1 acre = 10 square chains

The End

Acknowledgments

This book would not be in your hands were it not for my sister, Marianne Willingham Gilliam. I also owe a huge debt of thanks and gratitude to my agent and friend, Joann Davis, who has truly been a blessing in my work and in my life, and to my father, Charles Willingham, who never missed a chance to tell me I should write a book. Thank yous also go to Wes Griffin Jr. and Deborah Lukken Edge for sharing their artistic talents.

A sincere thank you to Toren Anderson, Laura Griffin, Laurie Johnson, Monique Kirby, Cindy Lukken, Louise Parham, and all of my priceless friends from "The Original Birthday Club" for their love and support during the compilation of this project. Big Mama is a tribute to each of them.

Very special thanks to my wonderful editor at Warner Books, Diana Baroni, and the wonderful people at Warner Books who have all been a delight to work with.

Finally, heartfelt thanks to my daughters, Elizabeth and Catherine, who make me want to create a home as nurturing and charming as Mrs. Dunwoody's, and to my husband, Peter John Lukken, who has always encouraged me to believe my dreams into being.

*The author would love
to hear from you.*

*You can reach her by e-mail at
www.MrsDunwoody.com*

*or send your letters to:
Miriam Lukken
P.O. Box 429
LaGrange, Georgia 30241*

Bibliography

Ashmore, Ruth, "Side Talks With Girls." *The Ladies Home Journal*, March 1897.

Brussat, Frederic and Mary Ann. *Spiritual Literacy*. New York: Touchstone, 1996.

Collier's Cyclopedia of Social and Commercial Information. New York: Collier Publishing Co., 1883.

Dodd, Marguerite. *America's Homemaking Book*. New York: Charles Scribner's Sons, 1957.

Emery, Carla. *The Encyclopedia of Country Living*. Seattle: Sasquatch Books, 1994.

Godey's Lady's Book magazine, March 1867.

Hausner, Julia. *Our Family Tree*. Secaucus, NJ: Poplar Books Inc., 1977.

Hill, Annabelle P. *Mrs. Hill's Practical Cookery and Receipt Book*. Columbia: University of South Carolina Press, 1995.

Hill, Professor Thomas E. *The Essential Handbook of Victorian Etiquette*. Chicago: Hill Standard Book Co., Publishers, 1888.

The Manners that Win: Compiled from the Latest Authorities. Minneapolis: Buckeye Publishing Co., 1880.

Mendelson, Cheryl. *Home Comforts: The Art and Science of Keeping House*. New York: Scribner, 1999.

Post, Emily. *Etiquette*. New York: Funk and Wagnall's, 1945.

Sandbeck, Ellen. *Slug Bread and Beheaded Thistles*. New York: Broadway Books, 1995.

Schlereth, Thomas J. *Victorian America, Transformations in Everyday Life 1876-1915*. New York: HarperPerennial, 1991.

Washington, George. *Rules of Civility & Decent Behavior in Company and Conversation*, 1747.

Walkup, Janna C. *The Victorian Lady.* Eugene: Harvest House Publishers, 1998.

Wright, Julia McNair, *The Complete Home.* Philadelphia: J.C. McCurdy, 1879.

Various unpublished papers, memoirs, and letters in the private collection of Peter John Lukken.

Index

butterfly gardens, 206–208
Byron, Lord, 177

C

D

daily homekeeping routine, 9–12
   children and, 9, 11
   cleanup, 11–12
   early rising, 9
   for housemaids, 10
   order and, 9, 11
   rhythm of, 9
dairy foods, 84–85
Dandeneau, Denis, 152
death, *see* passing over
Declaration of Independence, 22
deodorizing a room, 29–30
depression, 167
Dessert for Unexpected Guests, 75
diarrhea, 167
Dickinson, Emily, 5
"dining" not "eating," 118
   under no circumstances…, 119
dinner conversation, 113–14
dinner parties, 102
   rules of precedence at, 130
domestic calendar, 12–19
   accessories, 15–16
   cheap paint, 18
   daily cleaning chores, 13–14
   day-of-the-week chores, 14
   habit and order, 13
   hoarding and, 15
   homekeeping notebook and, 13
   monthly cleaning chores, 14–15
   notes for, 17
   routine and, 12–13
   seasonal cleaning chores, 15–19
   weekly cleaning chores, 14
   whitewash and, 18
domestic chemistry, 158–61
Donne, John, 141
drain declogger, 26
dry hair, 159
dry measures, 244
dry shampoo, 159
dull hair, 159
Dunwoody, Caroline, ix–xiii, 239
   as "Big Mama," xi–xii
   described, x
   home of, xiii
   "method and manner" of, xii
   note to children, xix–xx
   receipt book of, ix
   as widow, x
Dunwoody, Judge Charles Spalding, x, 38, 65, 72, 115, 135, 137, 151
dusting, 30–32

E

Ecclesiastes, 115
eggs, 84–85
Eliot, George, 136
Emerson, Ralph Waldo, 20–21
entertaining, 99–123
   common sense, 113, 117
   "dining" not "eating," 118
   guest books, 121–23
   holidays, 119

Mint Julep, Captain Clementine's, 78
Miss Lucinda's lemon furniture
polish, 26
Miss Lucinda's Lemon Ice Water,
75
Miss Olympia's oatmeal bath,
165–66
Miss Sallie Anne:
    all-purpose household cleaner,
        25
    laundry directions, 51–64
    restoring whiteness to
        scorched linen, 59
    starch recipe, 59–60
    succotash recipe, 69
molding clay for children,
    82–83
money, 178
mopping, 30–32
mosquitoes, 43
most important words, 180
moths, 44
Muffins, Mammie's, 72–73

N

nasty-chore cleaner, 25
nausea, 166

O

oatmeal bath, 165–66
odors, 6

controlling, 29–30
    deodorizing a room, 29–30
outdoor parties, 102

P

pace of life, vii
paint, cheap, 18
parties, 100–14
    buffet table, 111–12
    chores and details, 108–109
    dinner conversations, 113–14
    guest list, 103
    menus, 103–105
    planning, 100–101
    serving wine, 114
    table appointments, 105–107
    table setting and seating,
        109–11
    tea, 120
    types of, 101–103
passing over, 150–54
    condolence letter, 145,
        153–54
    plan of action, 151, 153
    poem about, 152
patent leather, 58
Pecan Pie, Ambrosial, 71
pepper bath for the feet, 166–67
perfume, geranium, 161
Philippines, 146
picnics, 102–103
Pie, Cut and Come Again, 72
Piecrust, Mammie Jane's, 71–72
planning notes for a superior day,
    19–22